TICK ...
TICK ...
TICK ...
TICK ...
TICK ...
TICK ...
TICK ...
TICK ...
TICK ...
TICK ...
TICK ...
TICK ...
TICK ...
TICK ...
TICK ...
TICK ...
TICK ...
TICK ...
TICK ...
TICK ...
TICK ...
TICK ...
TICK ...
TICK ...
TICK ...
TICK ...
TICK ...
TICK ...
TICK ...

The Way of the Master
Minute

A one-minute, one-year devotional ... for the busy Christian

TICK ...
TICK ...
TICK ...
TICK ...
TICK ...
TICK ...
TICK ...
TICK ...
TICK ...
TICK ...
TICK ...
TICK ...
TICK ...
TICK ...
TICK ...
TICK ...
TICK ...
TICK ...
TICK ...
TICK ...
TICK ...
TICK ...
TICK ...
TICK ...
TICK ...
TICK ...

**Kirk Cameron
and Ray Comfort**

The Way of the Master
Minute

**A one-minute,
one-year devotional
... for the busy
Christian**

Bridge-Logos
Gainesville, Florida 32614

Bridge-Logos

Gainesville, FL 32614 USA

The Way of the Master Minute
by Ray Comfort and Kirk Cameron

Printed in the United States of America.

Library of Congress Catalog Card Number: Pending
International Standard Book Number: 0-88270-161-4

Scriptures in the book are from *The Evidence Bible*

Photos by Carol Scott, CJ Studio, Covina, CA
www.cj-studio.com

G1.316.N.m601.352100

Dedication

To our faithful friends,
Stuart and Carol Scott,
whose wonderful photos adorn these pages.
We thank God for the day
He brought you into our lives.

Foreword

It was during the writing of this book that we rediscovered an incredible truth. We began to understand afresh that a great key to unlocking truths from the Word of God is to have a certain disciplined "attitude." Imagine that you have a metal detector that needs a battery to operate, but for some reason you run it over the ground without the battery. Understandably, you end up losing interest because you don't uncover any valuable metal. But the moment to put a battery into the detector, the dynamic radically changes. You have a sense of excitement as you find precious metal, and that energizes you to search for more.

When you read the Bible, your "attitude" is the battery. You have to deliberately put a particular attitude into your detector mind. Here is the mindset that will have you excitedly uncovering precious biblical truths—run your eyes over the Scriptures as though you had to write your own

The Way of the Master Minute book; you *have* to find something precious every time you read the Bible. That means you will diligently run the detector over and over familiar ground. Have a pen ready to write down what you uncover. It will take discipline to keep that "looking intently" attitude, but it will be most rewarding. It won't be long until you excitedly say, "I rejoice at Your word as one who finds great treasure."[1]

Until the nets are full,

Kirk Cameron and Ray Comfort

---

[1] Psalm 119:162

TICK ...
TICK ...
TICK ...
TICK ...
TICK ...
TICK ...
TICK ...
TICK ...
TICK ...
TICK ...
TICK ...
TICK ...
TICK ...
TICK ...
TICK ...
TICK ...
TICK ...
TICK ...
TICK ...
TICK ...
TICK ...
TICK ...
TICK ...
TICK ...
TICK ...
TICK ...
TICK ...

Illegitimate Children

When we remove words like *sin,
repentance, judgment,* and *Hell* from our
message, we are in danger of preaching
"another Gospel." If it's not the *whole*
truth, it's no longer the truth at all. It
becomes illegitimate and produces
illegitimate children, who call God their
father, but still serve the devil. The great
key to making sure that we are never
guilty of this is to say with Paul, "In the
sight of God we speak in Christ." In
other words, the words we speak are
never dictated by a fear of offending
sinners on earth. Instead, they are
dictated by the fear of offending a holy
God in Heaven. Nothing compromises
truth like seeking the approval of men.
And nothing *ensures* the truth like
seeking the approval of Almighty God.

There goes another minute.
Gone forever. **Go share your faith
while you still have time.**

A Hot Summer's Day

Here are two scenarios. The first is: You are standing by the edge of a swimming pool on a hot summer's day. Your flesh is hot; the water's cold. It's not going to be pleasant when you first hit the water. The longer you hesitate, the harder it becomes. Your friends call out, "The water's fine. Come on. You can do it. Just dive in!" Now here's the second scenario: You are hesitating by the water's edge. Suddenly you see your beloved four-year-old sink beneath the water in front of you. He's drowning! Do you still think about the cold water? No! *Not for a second.* Every day 150,000 people sink into the cold waters of death. Do you need to be coaxed to dive in to reach them before they pass into eternity?

There goes another minute.
***Gone forever.* Go share your faith while you still have time.**

Compassionate Firefighter

Do you ever think about the reality of Hell? Jesus spoke more of Hell than He did of Heaven. Such thoughts can do us good if we are compassionate of heart. That will drive us to make a difference, and pull sinners from the fire, as the Scriptures tell us to. Think of a compassionate firefighter. He's diligent in training because he knows what fire can do to human beings. He may even make himself looks at horrific images of actual fire scenes. This helps him to cultivate sobriety in his heart. It helps him to see the seriousness of the task he has before him. Today let's meditate for a moment on the terrible fate of the unsaved, and then, with the help of God, pull them from the fire.

There goes another minute. *Gone forever*. Go share your faith while you still have time.

TICK ...
TICK ...
TICK ...
TICK ...
TICK ...
TICK ...
TICK ...
TICK ...
TICK ...
TICK ...
TICK ...
TICK ...
TICK ...
TICK ...
TICK ...
TICK ...
TICK ...
TICK ...
TICK ...
TICK ...
TICK ...
TICK ...
TICK ...
TICK ...

4

He Named the Beggar

Do you remember the story Jesus told of Lazarus and the rich man in Luke 16? Think about how He graphically described the horrors of eternal judgment. Think on how (when He began to tell this story) Jesus said, "There *was*," and actually *named* the beggar. We mustn't feed complacency by believing that the story is allegorical or just some sort of metaphor. There is a literal and terrifying place called Hell, and we need to daily remind ourselves of its existence. Perhaps today, you and I need to seek God in heartfelt prayer, expressing our thoughts about our attitudes toward the fate of the lost, and pleading with Him to deepen our concern.

There goes another minute.
Gone forever. **Go share your faith**
while you still have time.

TICK ...
TICK ...
TICK ...
TICK ...
TICK ...
TICK ...
TICK ...
TICK ...
TICK ...
TICK ...
TICK ...
TICK ...
TICK ...
TICK ...
TICK ...
TICK ...
TICK ...
TICK ...
TICK ...
TICK ...
TICK ...
TICK ...
TICK ...
TICK ...
TICK ...
TICK ...
TICK ...

The Salvation Army

Have you noticed the Salvation Army has barracks, soldiers, uniforms, and generals? General Booth formed it that way so that they would never forget that they are involved in spiritual conflict. Each of us can easily forget that fact. We wrestle not against flesh and blood. We are engaged in *spiritual* conflict. Are you inspired by the Captain of our Salvation? Are you doing battle today? Are you seeking the lost? Take up your weapons and fight the good fight of faith, because there will be no peace on this earth until the Prince of Peace comes at the sound of the last trumpet, blown by the very cavalry of Calvary.

**There goes another minute.
Gone forever. Go share your faith
while you still have time.**

6

Switch on Some Darkness

Jesus said, "But you shall receive *power* when the Holy Spirit comes on you; *and you shall be my witnesses.*" The Holy Spirit was given so that we might have power for the purpose of being witnesses of Christ. Are we daily seeking the lost and sharing the Gospel, or are we afraid to let our light shine before men because we know that men hate the light. Yet, it is a natural principle that when light shines, darkness flees. Darkness *cannot* overcome light. Try it. Switch on some darkness and see if the light leaves. Then try it the other way around. Today, let your light shine before men, and when you lay your head on your pillow tonight, you will be glad you did.

There goes another minute.
Gone forever. **Go share your faith while you still have time.**

TICK ...
TICK ...
TICK ...
TICK ...
TICK ...
TICK ...
TICK ...
TICK ...
TICK ...
TICK ...
TICK ...
TICK ...
TICK ...
TICK ...
TICK ...
TICK ...
TICK ...
TICK ...
TICK ...
TICK ...
TICK ...
TICK ...
TICK ...
TICK ...
TICK ...
TICK ...

Singing Songs in the Lifeboat

The Apostle Paul said, "For me to live means opportunities for Christ." Is there a zeal to share our faith burning in our bones? It's *more* than spending time in worship or prayer. Jesus said to "Go and *preach*." Prayer and worship are the basics of the Christian faith, but if we are not obediently *sharing* that faith, we are not fulfilling The Great Commission. Obedience is *better* than sacrifice. Without evangelistic zeal, we are like survivors of the Titanic, singing songs in the lifeboat while people are drowning. Singing songs is fine … *but not while people are drowning*. Let's put service with worship. Let's put legs to our prayers, and today seek to save those who will perish without the Savior.

There goes another minute. *Gone forever*. Go share your faith while you still have time.

Wings to the Feet of Service

The Bible says to put on "the breastplate of faith *and love ...*" In another place Scripture speaks of a breastplate of "righteousness." Righteousness without love is no defense against the enemy. The religious Pharisees had a form of righteousness, yet Jesus still called them sons of the devil. The Bible tells us that without love, we are nothing. Charles Spurgeon said, "Love should give wings to the feet of service, and strength to the arms of labor." So, if you are a Christian, today make sure your heart is guarded with the breastplate of righteousness, by never allowing sin to have any dwelling place in your heart. Then let love have its way—put wings to the feet of service, and go and take the Gospel to this dying world.

There goes another minute.
Gone forever. **Go share your faith**
while you still have time.

TICK ...

Formula for Success

TICK ...

TICK ...
TICK ...
TICK ...
TICK ...
TICK ...
TICK ...
TICK ...
TICK ...
TICK ...
TICK ...
TICK ...
TICK ...
TICK ...
TICK ...

Here is the biblical formula for success for the Christian. Meditate on God's Word *every* day. Have you ever gone for a day when you have been too busy or have forgotten to read the Bible? Have you ever gone a day when you have been too busy or have forgotten to feed your stomach? Which comes first—your Bible or your belly? Be like Job, who "esteemed the words of His mouth more than [his] necessary food." You have God's promise in the first Psalm that if you mediate on the Law of God both day and night, then you will be fruitful, and "whatever you do will prosper." That's not just your marriage or your job; it's also your evangelistic efforts. Say to yourself: No Bible, no breakfast. No read, no feed.

TICK ...
TICK ...
TICK ...

TICK ...

**There goes another minute.
Gone forever. Go share your faith
while you still have time.**

TICK ...
TICK ...
TICK ...
TICK ...
TICK ...
TICK ...

Ride Out the Hurricane

Back in 1969, twenty-four people decided to ignore warnings that Hurricane Camille was heading for Mississippi. They were going to ride it out. Twenty-three of them died in the wrath of that hurricane. What a terrible tragedy. If they had taken the warning seriously, they wouldn't have lost their precious lives. The cross is a terrible warning of the fierce hurricane of God's wrath, which no one can "ride out" on Judgment Day. We must never tire of *warning* every man "that we might present every man perfect in Christ Jesus." He is their only hope. They must, as the Bible says "kiss the Son, lest He be angry, and perish from the way, when His wrath is kindled but a little."

**There goes another minute.
Gone forever. Go share your faith
while you still have time.**

God's Perspective

As far as the world is concerned, there are many people who are morally good. However, the Bible says that there is none good. Not one. Romans chapter 3 gives us God's perspective of humanity: *No one* understands or seeks after God. *All* have turned away from Him. They have together become filthy. There is *no one* who does good, not even one. The world may consider it a good thing when a celebrity gives millions of dollars to charity. God, however, sees the *motive* for the act, which may be guilt for a past sinful lifestyle. As long as the world is left without the light of God's Law, it will be in the dark as to the true meaning of the word "good." Biblically, it means "moral perfection."

There goes another minute.
Gone forever. **Go share your faith while you still have time.**

Merely to Obtain Dirt

When David was faced with Goliath, he *ran* toward him. We have a goliath task in front of us, and we too must run into the battle for the lost. History shows us that soldiers have rushed into battle merely to obtain dirt. Many have given their lives to get back a hill in Vietnam, Korea, or Israel—a hill that may be returned to the enemy through peace negotiations twenty years later. Their costly efforts proved to be futile. Our labor, however, is not in vain. It's eternal, and it's the most noble battle in which we could be involved. Listen to Scripture: "Wherefore, my beloved brethren, be steadfast, unmovable, always abounding in the work of the Lord, forasmuch as you know that your labor is not vain in the Lord."

There goes another minute.
Gone forever. **Go share your faith while you still have time.**

TICK ...
TICK ...
TICK ...
TICK ...
TICK ...
TICK ...
TICK ...
TICK ...
TICK ...
TICK ...
TICK ...
TICK ...
TICK ...
TICK ...
TICK ...
TICK ...
TICK ...
TICK ...
TICK ...
TICK ...
TICK ...
TICK ...
TICK ...
TICK ...
TICK ...
TICK ...

Better Job, Bigger House

What are our desires? Do we want to have a better job, a bigger house, thicker carpet, and more money? Are we controlled by the lust of the flesh, the lust of the eyes, and the pride of life? Or have we been transformed from the way of this world by "the renewing of [our] mind?" When that happens, we are told that we "may prove what is that good, and acceptable, and perfect will of God." So, ask yourself, "Are my desires in line with God's desires?" Am I "not willing that any should perish, but that all should come to repentance?" That's God's perfect will. Is it yours? When it is—when your desires match His and you delight yourself in the Lord, you are promised that He will give you those heart's desires.

There goes another minute.
Gone forever. Go share your faith
while you still have time.

The Sergeant Major

As Christians, we have enlisted in the Army of God. How loudly then does the sergeant major of our conscience need to shout to bring us to attention? If we move out of order, do we hear His voice? A good soldier won't even wait for the voice of a sergeant major to call him into line. If by chance he gets out of step, he makes an immediate correction. Is there something in our lives that's out of step with God? Have we unforgiveness in our hearts? Then forgive or you will not be forgiven. Do we lack love enough to reach out to the lost? Then we must ask God to pour His love through us, or we have no biblical grounds to think we are saved. Love could never sit in passivity while sinners sink into Hell.

**There goes another minute.
Gone forever. Go share your faith
while you still have time.**

TICK ...
TICK ...
TICK
TICK ...
TICK ...

A Straight-Shooter with the Pistol

TICK ...
TICK ...
TICK ...
TICK ...
TICK ...
TICK ...
TICK ...
TICK ...
TICK ...
TICK ...
TICK ...
TICK ...
TICK ...
TICK ...

There is no such thing as small sin. Perhaps when Judas stole from the bag, he just took a little here and there. But remember, it only takes a small hole to sink a great ocean liner. The Bible tells us that God is righteous. Righteousness can no more be separated from His nature than the water from the ocean. We must strive to always have good consciences toward God, not only for our own sakes, but also for the sake of the lost. If you are a soldier of Christ and you want to be used by God, make sure that you keep your heart free from all sin, even those that most consider "small" sins. *It is a true principle: If I am not a straight-shooter with a pistol, it's certain that He won't let me near the cannon* .

TICK ...
TICK ...
TICK ...
TICK ...
TICK ...
TICK ...
TICK ...

There goes another minute. *Gone forever*. Go share your faith while you still have time.

TICK ...
TICK ...
TICK ...
TICK ...
TICK ...
TICK ...
TICK ...

Practice What You Preach

Do you ever *practice* what you preach? Perhaps you could practice with your mirror. Make sure you are alone, and ask it a friendly, "How are you doing? Did you get one of these?" Say, "It's a Gospel tract. What do you think happens after someone dies? Do you believe in Heaven and Hell?" Keep practicing until you shake off self-consciousness. Think of how a child begins to walk. Each step is at first deliberate and stumbling. He lacks grace. But in time, one step just follows the other without a second thought. Aim to get to that place. Learn to go through the Ten Commandments as Jesus did; then preach the cross. The Bible says to always be ready to give a "reason for the hope that's within you." There's no greater calling.

There goes another minute. *Gone forever*. Go share your faith while you still have time.

TICK ...
TICK ...
TICK ...
TICK ...
TICK ...
TICK ...
TICK ...
TICK ...
TICK ...
TICK ...
TICK ...
TICK ...
TICK ...
TICK ...
TICK ...
TICK ...
TICK ...
TICK ...
TICK ...
TICK ...
TICK ...
TICK ...
TICK ...
TICK ...
TICK ...
TICK ...
TICK ...
TICK ...
TICK ...

17

Put in What They Leave Out

Go to the Internet and type in the search word, "Evangelism," or "How to be saved." Go to the sites listed and find their Gospel messages. See if there is a *sound* biblical Gospel presentation. Do they open up with the Law, and warn of Judgment Day and Hell? Do they preach the cross, the resurrection, repentance, and faith? Is Jesus presented as the answer to life's problems or as the Savior from sin? Watch Christian TV and analyze their Gospel presentation. If it is lacking content, then learn from their mistakes. Don't have a condescending attitude, but determine to make sure you *always* put in what they leave out, and take a moment to pray for them, that they return to the biblical Gospel presentation.

**There goes another minute.
Gone forever. Go share your faith
while you still have time.**

A Masked Burglar

Have you ever seen a masked burglar (in a movie) creep through someone's house? The fact that you can't see his face produces fear, but somehow the fear dissipates the moment the mask is ripped from his head, and you see who he is. Why are we afraid to reach out to the lost? Isn't it because we fear *rejection*? What then is behind the mask? It's human pride. We don't want anyone to think badly of us. The Bible says, "Every one that is proud in heart is an abomination to the Lord." Seeing what's under the mask will help us to dissipate our fears. Repent of the sin of pride. Then go in humility and reach those who may be snatched into everlasting Hell.

There goes another minute.
Gone forever. **Go share your faith**
while you still have time.

TICK ...
TICK ...
TICK ...
TICK ...
TICK ...
TICK ...
TICK ...
TICK ...
TICK ...
TICK ...
TICK ...
TICK ...
TICK ...
TICK ...
TICK ...
TICK ...
TICK ...
TICK ...
TICK ...
TICK ...
TICK ...
TICK ...
TICK ...
TICK ...

Virtues of a Firefighter

Imagine that you are sound asleep in bed, and unbeknown to you, your house is on fire. There's a fire station next door. What virtues would you like the firefighters to have? Wouldn't you want them to have alertness, strength, training, courage, diligence, and concern for others? Do you and I possess those necessary strengths? Are we concerned for others? Are we sober, alert, and diligent? Are we horrified at the thought of any human being ending up in Hell? Are we strengthening ourselves through prayer and faith in Jesus Christ? Are we diligently training to reach out to the lost? If we don't study the subject and learn how to speak to the unsaved, we won't be ready when God gives us an opportunity, and it may never come again.

**There goes another minute.
Gone forever. Go share your faith
while you still have time.**

It Rang in Their Ears

Do you feel frustrated by Christians who have no concern for the lost? Do you wonder if they have ever opened the Book of Acts? Every corner that the early Church turned, it preached Christ crucified. They were motivated by The Great Commission. It rang in their ears. Jesus said to go, and so they went . . . and so should we. One way to do this is to get yourself into the mentality that today is going to be your last day on this earth. Your very last. Tomorrow you will be in eternity. It's a scary thought, but ask yourself what you would do with your last precious hours of time? Hopefully, you would become "eternity minded," and you would want to desperately seek and save the lost like a dying man. Be like that daily.

There goes another minute.
Gone forever. Go share your faith
while you still have time.

TICK ...
TICK ...
TICK ...
TICK ...
TICK ...
TICK ...
TICK ...
TICK ...
TICK ...
TICK ...
TICK ...
TICK ...
TICK ...
TICK ...
TICK ...
TICK ...
TICK ...
TICK ...
TICK ...
TICK ...
TICK ...
TICK ...
TICK ...
TICK ...
TICK ...
TICK ...
TICK ...

21

We Know Hell Exists

In the story of Lazarus and the Rich Man, the rich man's heart was so hard that he let Lazarus starve at his gate. He had a heart of stone . . . until he found himself in Hell. It took Hell to soften him to a point were he was at least concerned for his loved ones. We *know* that Hell exists. Are we therefore concerned about the fate of our unsaved loved ones? How about our friends and neighbors? Is our love deep enough to even be concerned for the eternal welfare of *strangers*? It should be. If we are born again, the love of God *has* been shed abroad in our hearts by the Holy Spirit, and that love will warn them of a real Hell and of the mercy of God in Christ.

There goes another minute.
Gone forever. Go share your faith
while you still have time.

Confronting the Hypocrite

In Luke 16:14, Jesus said to the covetous Pharisees, "You are they who justify themselves before men." Not only did they *seek* justification in the sight of men, but no doubt, they *attained* it. In other words, if we looked at a Pharisee, we would say, "There goes a righteous person. There goes someone who is right with God." But Jesus then said that God saw their thought-life, and that of which man thinks highly is an abomination in the sight of God. When you need to confront someone who is a hypocrite, do what Jesus did—open up the spiritual nature of the Law so that sin will be seen in its true light.

There goes another minute.
Gone forever. Go share your faith
while you still have time.

TICK ...
TICK ...
TICK ...
TICK ...
TICK ...
TICK ...
TICK ...
TICK ...
TICK ...
TICK ...
TICK ...
TICK ...
TICK ...
TICK ...
TICK ...
TICK ...
TICK ...
TICK ...
TICK ...
TICK ...
TICK ...
TICK ...
TICK ...
TICK ...
TICK ...

About What Should We Testify?

In the story of Lazarus and the Rich man, we are told that when the rich man was in Hell, he pleaded with Abraham to have someone go to his father's house to *testify* to his family. About *what* should they testify? Imagine that the rich man has appeared to *you* and is speaking at this moment. His clothes are smoking with heat. His terrified eyes are aflame with fire. He wants you to *testify* to his loved ones. What should you say to them—"There's a God-shaped vacuum in your heart that only God can fill"? Of course not. He would have you warn them of the terrible reality of Hell, and tell them to turn from sin and flee to the Savior. That's our commission. Don't be distracted from such a sobering task.

**There goes another minute.
Gone forever. Go share your faith
while you still have time.**

Friendship Evangelism

If you saw that someone was about to drink deadly poison, what would you do? Would you seek to warn him? Wouldn't there be a sense of urgency on your part to stop him from putting that cup to his lips? Would you passively become friends with him and let him drink as you talk with him about other things? "Friendship evangelism," which never warns people of any danger, is the ultimate betrayal of trust. How can we call ourselves that person's "friend?" Friends don't let friends go to Hell. Who do you know who isn't saved? Why are you hesitating to warn them? How will you feel if today he or she is snatched into eternity and gone forever? Don't put off what you know you must do.

There goes another minute.
Gone forever. **Go share your faith while you still have time.**

TICK ...
TICK ...
TICK ...
TICK ...
TICK ...
TICK ...
TICK ...
TICK ...
TICK ...
TICK ...
TICK ...
TICK ...
TICK ...
TICK ...
TICK ...
TICK ...
TICK ...
TICK ...
TICK ...
TICK ...
TICK ...
TICK ...
TICK ...
TICK ...
TICK ...
TICK ...

25

Instant Memories

Do you ever smell a smell or hear a song that brings instant memories from the past to your mind? Sometimes the memory is pleasant; sometimes it's not, but whatever the case, such memories should remind us that everything we have ever done has been logged into the human memory. There is a complete file of every thought, word, and deed. What a fearful thing for the unsaved. On the day of Judgment, sinful thoughts, words, and deeds will come out as damning evidence of their guilt before a holy God and a Law they have violated a multitude of times. May we remember this day that it's a fearful thing for the ungodly to fall into the hands of the Living God.

There goes another minute.
Gone forever. **Go share your faith while you still have time.**

If the Vehicle Lacks Fuel

Ask yourself who you know who isn't saved.
Without the blood of the Savior, those people
you are thinking of will one day be cast into
the Lake of Fire. How does that make you feel?
Does it make you want to reach them with the
Gospel? If we are lacking the fuels of
compassion and gratitude for our own
salvation, the task of sharing our faith will
become a chore. It will be a burden. If our
vehicle lacks fuel, we'll have to push it rather
than drive it. If we have to *push* the vehicle of
evangelism, it will be a tiresome task, while
driving it will be exhilarating. Without the gas
of gratitude, our attitude won't be an
enthusiastic, "I delight to do Your will," but a
begrudging, "I *have* to do Your will."

**There goes another minute.
Gone forever. Go share your faith
while you still have time.**

TICK
TICK
TICK
TICK
TICK
TICK
TICK
TICK
TICK
TICK
TICK
TICK
TICK
TICK
TICK
TICK
TICK
TICK
TICK
TICK
TICK
TICK
TICK
TICK
TICK
TICK
TICK

The Garden Experience

Have you had a Garden of Gethsemane experience? It was in a garden where Adam first said, "Not Your will, but *mine* be done," and it was in a garden where Jesus fell to His knees and prayed, "Not my will, but Yours be done." At the time, His disciples were asleep; so when it comes to seeking the lost, don't be discouraged if those around you are asleep. Simply get on your knees and say, "Father, the thought of sharing the Gospel makes me sweat great drops of blood in fear. Yet not my will, but Yours be done." Make it so real that the next time you are tempted to do you own will, you will remember your agonizing Gethsemane experience—that you live for His will and good pleasure, not your you own.

There goes another minute.
Gone forever. **Go share your faith**
while you still have time.

Relive the Emotions

Do you ever consider the *reason* for your coming to the Savior? Was there a thorough knowledge of sin? Where did it come from? Try to relive the emotions of the day of your conversion. Did the Law condemn you? Did it send you to the cross? What part did your conscience play in your salvation? Did it suddenly come alive, or had it been speaking to you for some time? What do you think was your greatest sin? Were you afraid of God? Was there a knowledge of future punishment? Most of all, *think of what would have happened to you if you had died in your sins.* Then express your gratitude to God for that cross, where His great love was poured out for you, and let it motivate you to do His will and reach the lost.

There goes another minute.
Gone forever. **Go share your faith while you still have time.**

TICK ...
TICK ...
TICK ...

29

TICK ...
TICK ...
TICK ...

Paul's "Good" Test

TICK ...
TICK ...
TICK ...
TICK ...
TICK ...
TICK ...
TICK ...
TICK ...
TICK ...
TICK ...
TICK ...
TICK ...
TICK ...
TICK ...
TICK ...

Have you ever noticed in Romans chapter 2 that the Apostle Paul used God's Law to bring to knowledge of sin? He asked, "You, therefore, who teach another, do you not teach yourself? You who preach that a man should not steal, do you steal? You who say, 'Do not commit adultery,' do you commit adultery? You who abhor idols, do you rob temples? You who make your boast in the Law, do you dishonor God through breaking the law?" He *personalized* the Commandments. He appealed to his hearer's conscience. This is also what Jesus did. There's a good reason for doing this. The Law prepares the heart for grace. It brings the knowledge of sin. It magnifies the love of God in Christ. So, do the same. Imitate Jesus today.

**There goes another minute.
Gone forever. Go share your faith
while you still have time.**

TICK ...
TICK ...
TICK ...
TICK ...
TICK ...
TICK ...
TICK ...

Building Relationships

Most of us would agree with the philosophy of what is known in Christian circles as "friendship evangelism." This is the thought that we should befriend someone and then build a relationship with them *before* we witness to them. There's nothing wrong with that. It's good to build relationships, but the question arises as to *how long* we develop the friendship *before* we speak about his or her relationship with God. Jesus built a relationship with the woman at the well in just a few minutes. What happens to your unsaved friend if he dies while you are taking the time to build a friendship with him? He will go to Hell for eternity if he dies without knowing the forgiveness of sins. So, don't wait for too long.

**There goes another minute.
Gone forever. Go share your faith
while you still have time.**

TICK
TICK
TICK
TICK
TICK
TICK
TICK
TICK
TICK
TICK
TICK
TICK
TICK
TICK
TICK
TICK
TICK
TICK
TICK
TICK
TICK
TICK
TICK
TICK
TICK

Witnessing the Strangers

Who are some of the hardest people to whom we witness? Aren't they our friends and relations? Why is this? It's because if we witness to someone with whom we have a good relationship and offend him, we risk losing that relationship. But if we witness to a stranger and we offend him, we have lost nothing at all. So, it makes sense to make it easier for ourselves by learning to witness to strangers. We should make sharing the Gospel with strangers a way of life. Doing it regularly will help to make it easier for us to be bold with those we hold dear. Whoever we speak to, we must develop a sense of urgency, knowing that the person to whom we are speaking may not have tomorrow. Today is the day of salvation.

**There goes another minute.
Gone forever. Go share your faith
while you still have time.**

Go Your Way

Never be discouraged if someone suddenly wants to terminate a witnessing conversation. Paul's conversation with Felix the Governor was suddenly terminated. Felix said, "Go your way..." The Bible tells us *why* Felix did that. He was trembling. The Law has that effect on those that are guilty. Paul reasoned about *righteousness* (which is of the Law) and *judgment* (which is by the Law). He spoke about *"temperance,"* and the guilty governor tremble and terminated the conversation. The Apostle may not have seen him trembling, and been disheartened. So never be discouraged when a conversation suddenly ends. Agitation or anger is a sign that something is going on in the heart. Don't give up on the person. Use the secret weapon of closet prayer. God can continue speaking to him, even if you can't.

There goes another minute.
Gone forever. Go share your faith
while you still have time.

TICK ...
TICK ...
TICK ...
TICK ...
TICK ...
TICK ...
TICK ...
TICK ...
TICK ...
TICK ...
TICK ...
TICK ...
TICK ...
TICK ...
TICK ...
TICK ...
TICK ...
TICK ...
TICK ...
TICK ...
TICK ...
TICK ...
TICK ...
TICK ...
TICK ...
TICK ...
TICK ...
TICK ...

The Comfort of the Fire Truck

Perhaps you don't have an "out-going" personality. Perhaps you are shy, and you like to keep to yourself. A firefighter may have the type of personality that likes to stay alone in the comfort of a fire truck and read books, but if he wants to do what he knows he should, he must change that attitude. So, step out of the truck. Make an effort today to greet at least two complete strangers. When you walk into the grocery store, the gas station, school, or work, practice being friendly with people you don't know. Make yourself say, "Hi. How are you doing?" Try it and you will see that it really isn't difficult at all. Then be bold. Offer them a tract, and run if you must. Better to give it and run than not give it at all.

There goes another minute. *Gone forever*. Go share your faith while you still have time.

Prepared for Battle

The Bible says that we wrestle against dark demonic forces, and that we are to stand against them fully clothed for battle. We are to "wear" truth. When deceit enters, so does the devil. We "give place" to him when truth leaves. We are also to wear the breastplate of righteousness and take the helmet of salvation, the sword of the Spirit, and the shield of faith. Most Christians do that. However, many ignore that we are told to have our feet shod with the "preparation" of the Gospel of Peace. What does that mean? How do we prepare our feet for battle? We pray. We pray particularly about the lost. We pray for wisdom, for the words that will turn them from a path that is taking them to Hell, and then we put legs to our prayers and go and seek them.

There goes another minute.
Gone forever. Go share your faith
while you still have time.

TICK ...
TICK ...
TICK ...
TICK ...
TICK ...
TICK ...
TICK ...
TICK ...
TICK ...
TICK ...
TICK ...
TICK ...
TICK ...
TICK ...
TICK ...
TICK ...
TICK ...
TICK ...
TICK ...
TICK ...
TICK ...
TICK ...
TICK ...
TICK ...
TICK ...
TICK ...
TICK ...

35

An Open Invitation

Do you ever ask God for wisdom? The Bible gives us an open invitation. It says, "If any of you lacks wisdom, let him ask of God, who gives to all liberally…" If you have wisdom, you will think right, say right, and do right. It will save you a lot of pain. When Solomon asked for wisdom instead of long life, it so pleased God that He gave Him both. We should soak our souls in the Book of Proverbs—it's a power-pack of wisdom. We can also gain wisdom through the experiences of others. In Ephesians 1:17 the Apostle Paul asks that we be given "the *spirit* of wisdom." We are told, "He that wins souls is *wise*." Live in *the* spirit of wisdom. Live to reach the lost.

**There goes another minute.
Gone forever. Go share your faith
while you still have time.**

Tides of Revival

Have you ever studied the moon? Its purpose is to be a light in the night, and it gives light by reflecting the sun. The Church is like the moon. We reflect the light of God in the darkness of this sinful world. But there is another side to the moon. It has an invisible gravitational pull that affects the *tides* of the earth. With God's help, the Church can affect the tides of revival on this earth. Revival is merely the Church doing what it should. Can you imagine what would happen if every Christian became *passionate* about sharing his or her faith—if every Christian said "For me to live is Christ" and they witnessed *biblically*? We would have revival. So today, pray for laborers, and encourage other Christians to reach out to the lost.

Praying For Laborers

Jesus said, "The harvest truly is great, but the laborers are few; therefore pray the Lord of the harvest to send out laborers into His harvest." Are you doing that? Are you *praying* for laborers? If you don't share your faith with others, then you won't pray for laborers. Your guilt will stop you; and so the devil gets a double victory. Not only do you not reach out to the lost, but you don't even pray for others to do so. Change that today. Cry out to the Lord of the Harvest to raise up fearless and faithful Christians who will do nothing else but the will of God by obeying to The Great Commission. Then say with the prophet, "Here I am Lord; send me," and put legs to your prayers. Don't wait any longer.

**There goes another minute.
Gone forever. Go share your faith
while you still have time.**

Divine Encounters

What is the priority of your life? Look at Apostle Paul's. He said, "For if I preach the Gospel, I have nothing to boast of, for necessity is laid upon me; yes, woe is me if I do not preach the Gospel! ... I have made myself a servant to all, that I might win the more ... I have become all things to all men, that I might by all means save some." Is that your priority today? How are you going to do it? How are you going to "save some?" Are you going to be *looking* for a divine encounter, where God has prepared the heart of someone to whom you can speak? Are you praying for that? Are you going to leave a Gospel tract somewhere today? Whatever you do, do something today. Tomorrow may never come.

There goes another minute.
Gone forever. Go share your faith
while you still have time.

TICK ...
TICK ...
TICK ...
TICK ...
TICK ...
TICK ...
TICK ...
TICK ...
TICK ...
TICK ...
TICK ...
TICK ...
TICK ...
TICK ...
TICK ...
TICK ...
TICK ...
TICK ...
TICK ...
TICK ...
TICK ...
TICK ...
TICK ...
TICK ...
TICK ...
TICK ...
TICK ...
TICK ...

Taking the Initiative

Study how Jesus spoke to the woman at the well. *He went out of His way* to speak to her. *He* took the initiative. He didn't wait for her to bring up the things of God. We need to do the same. The world won't come to us and ask us about God. They love the darkness and hate the light— "neither will they come to the light, lest their deeds are exposed." So, determine to do what Jesus did. Go into all the world. Perhaps use a Gospel tract to bring up the subject. Hand it to someone and ask, "Did you get one of these?" Let curiosity do its work, and when they ask "What is it?" say, "It's a Gospel tract. Have you had a Christian background? What do you think happens after someone dies?" Do it. Today.

**There goes another minute.
Gone forever. Go share your faith
while you still have time.**

40

Isaiah Was Very Bold

The Bible says "But Isaiah is very bold and says: 'I was found by those who did not seek Me.'" Why was Isaiah "bold?" It was because he was saying that salvation was also for the Gentiles. Most Jews thought it was confined to Israel, and that's why they tried to kill Paul when he said that he was sent to the Gentiles[2]. But the promise of eternal life has *always* been universal. Isaiah 55:1 says, "Ho! *Everyone* who thirsts, come to the waters…" Joel 2:32 says, "*Whoever* calls on the name of the Lord shall be saved." The Gospel is for *all* humanity. That means your loved ones, your neighbors, your coworkers, and even your boss may be saved. So, be "very bold." Today, take the good news that Jesus Christ has abolished death to those who sit in the shadow of death.

TICK ...

Then Will I Teach

TICK ...

TICK ...

After David had sinned with Bathsheba and God used Nathan the prophet to expose his sin, the king cried, "Have mercy upon me, O God, according to Your lovingkindness; according to the multitude of Your tender mercies, blot out my transgressions." Our sins can be blotted out, not because of anything we have done, but because of the "multitude of [God's] tender mercies." Then David pleaded, "Wash me thoroughly from my iniquity, and cleanse me from my sin." Notice the word "thoroughly." Have we been washed "thoroughly" or is there some dirty little secret sin still clinging to our flesh? Being clean in God's sight is the great key to reaching to lost. David's then prayed, "*Then* I will teach transgressors Your ways, and sinners shall be converted to You."

**There goes another minute.
Gone forever. Go share your faith
while you still have time.**

Finding God's Will

How do you find God's will for your life? Just "Present your body as a living sacrifice, holy, acceptable to God, *which is* your reasonable service. And do not be conformed to this world, but be transformed by the renewing of your mind, that you may prove what *is* that good and acceptable and perfect will of God."[3] So there you have it. Lay down your life in service of God; be holy—be *transformed* by renewing your mind. When that happens, you will suddenly say, "People are going to Hell. God doesn't want any to perish—that's what the cross was all about. He wants me to reach them with the Gospel, so that's what I will do." It's very simple. So, today do that. Do the will of God. Seek and save the lost.

There goes another minute.
Gone forever. **Go share your faith
while you still have time.**

Negative Thoughts

The Scriptures tell us that we don't wrestle against flesh and blood, but against a spiritual world.[4] We are surrounded by demonic forces that bombard our minds with fears and negative thoughts when it comes to seeking the lost. If you think that those fears are from your own mind, you won't bother using the full armor of God as listed in Ephesians chapter 6, but if you believe the Scriptures—that you have a very real enemy, then you will see that you need a very real armor. Despite this, most of us forget that the spiritual realm is the *source* of fearful thoughts. So, do what the Bible says, and put on the *whole* armor of God. When the negative thoughts come, resist them "steadfast in the faith,"[5] and then seek and save the lost with all your heart.

**There goes another minute.
Gone forever. Go share your faith
while you still have time.**

TICK ...
TICK ...
TICK ...
TICK ...
TICK ...
TICK ...
TICK ...
TICK ...
TICK ...
TICK ...
TICK ...
TICK ...
TICK ...
TICK ...
TICK ...
TICK ...
TICK ...
TICK ...
TICK ...
TICK ...
TICK ...
TICK ...
TICK ...
TICK ...
TICK ...
TICK ...

Keeping Courage

One of the enemy's most powerful weapons (if not *the* most powerful weapon) is fear. Fear will make you want to stop doing battle to reach the lost, and to retreat into the comfort of the barracks. Think of the word, "dis-courage." Satan wants to rid you of your *courage*. So soldier of Christ, when you fight the good fight of faith, make sure you have a sensitive ear to subtle discouraging thoughts, and recognize where they are coming from. The great key is to have a once and for all Gethsemane experience—where you lay down your will and say, "God, I want to do Your will in my life—and Your will is that none perish." Then never be discouraged from the battle. This war is far too important to even *consider* retreating.

**There goes another minute.
Gone forever. Go share your faith
while you still have time.**

That's Your Interpretation

When you point out a Bible verse about the reality of Judgment Day, do you ever have people say something like, "That's just *your* interpretation!"? If that happens, quote Luke 13:3 to them. Read it to them and ask them to give *their* interpretation. Get it into their hearts. It's quick and powerful and sharper than any two-edged sword. Also, never be concerned when sinners tell you that the Bible has changed or that it is filled with mistakes or that they don't believe it. The Bible was given as a lamp to our path, and it only gives us light when we approach it with childlike faith and humility of heart. So, don't worry about their unbelief. Get it into their hearts. It won't return void. Then pray that God brings it to life at the right time.

**There goes another minute.
Gone forever. Go share your faith
while you still have time.**

TICK ...
TICK ...
TICK ...
TICK ...
TICK ...
TICK ...
TICK ...
TICK ...
TICK ...
TICK ...
TICK ...
TICK ...
TICK ...
TICK ...
TICK ...
TICK ...
TICK ...
TICK ...
TICK ...
TICK ...
TICK ...
TICK ...
TICK ...
TICK ...
TICK ...
TICK ...

The Terror of Combat

Imagine that you are a soldier who is about to enter combat for the first time. You *have* to enter the battlefield or be shot as a cowardly deserter. Get into that state of mind that you *really* believe that the enemy wants to kill you. He passionately wants to see *your* blood spilled on the ground. Let your mind's eye make this experience so real that you can actually feel the terror of being shot to death. Think now how soberly and diligently you would be as you put on your body armor and prepare your weapons, and how thankful you would be for your training. Keep that sober state of mind and carefully read Ephesians 6:10-20. There you will find your battle instructions for the real *war* that has eternal repercussions. Then make sure you are always battle-ready.

**There goes another minute.
Gone forever. Go share your faith
while you still have time.**

TICK ...
TICK ...
TICK ...
TICK ...
TICK ...
TICK ...
TICK ...
TICK ...
TICK ...
TICK ...
TICK ...
TICK ...
TICK ...
TICK ...
TICK ...
TICK ...
TICK ...
TICK ...
TICK ...
TICK ...
TICK ...
TICK ...
TICK ...
TICK ...
TICK ...

47

The Mystery of Existence

When Hugh Hefner was asked, "If you could ask God one question, what would it be?" he replied, "Oh, I think the one question I'd really like to know is the question related to an afterlife. And the other question is the meaning of it all." The godly don't need to ask these questions, because the Bible gives us the answers. The afterlife is no mystery ... unless we *make* it a mystery by refusing to believe the truth of Scripture. Those who refuse to believe are left without any reason for existence. One well-known actor said that when he dies, his last words will be, "That was nice. I wonder what that was all about?" What a tragedy, and what a terrible awakening they will get when they stand before a holy Creator. We must warn them.

There goes another minute.
Gone forever. **Go share your faith while you still have time.**

Asking God One Question

If you (as a Christian) were allowed to ask God one question face to face, what would it be? Perhaps we could ask how and when we will leave this life. Is that a frightening thought to you? Perhaps we should meditate on it, because it would help us to make sure that we inject eternity into the temporal. Thinking about life and its transient nature can help us to think about death and eternal implications for the lost, and that's what matters most. *We* are safe in the arms of Jesus, but they are in their sins and if they die in that state, they will go to Hell forever. We must therefore make every moment count in our efforts to reach them with the Gospel, and if we are not doing that, we must begin doing it today.

There goes another minute.
Gone forever. Go share your faith
while you still have time.

TICK ...
TICK ...
TICK ...
TICK ...
TICK ...
TICK ...
TICK ...
TICK ...
TICK ...
TICK ...
TICK ...
TICK ...
TICK ...
TICK ...
TICK ...
TICK ...
TICK ...
TICK ...
TICK ...
TICK ...
TICK ...
TICK ...
TICK ...
TICK ...
TICK ...
TICK ...
TICK ...
TICK ...

49

Hell is a Good Reason

It's unwise to give an unrepentant sinner the message of God's forgiveness unless he shows some evident concern about his salvation. For example, lust is such a blinding and powerful sin, a man will not want to let it go unless he becomes convinced that it's in his best interest to do so. *Hell is a very good reason to do so.* So, use the analogy of lust being like a sparkling stick of dynamite in a child's hand. He loves the sparkle and holds it close with great delight. He doesn't realize that it will kill him. Lust sparkles before the face of the unsaved, but it will bring terrible destruction. The Bible says that "when it has conceived, it brings forth sin: and sin, when it is finished, brings forth death." Without the understanding that he is in danger, sin will damn him forever.

**There goes another minute.
Gone forever. Go share your faith
while you still have time.**

He Told Me Everything

We are told in Scripture that there is joy in Heaven when one sinner finds a place of repentance. After Jesus spoke to the woman at the well we are told that "many of the Samaritans of that city believed in Him because of the word of the woman who testified 'He told me all that I ever did.'"[6] What did she mean by saying, "He told me all that I ever did"? The answer is clear. He spoke to her about her transgression of the Seventh Commandment.[7] What was the result? Many of the Samaritans of that city believed in Jesus. How can we best imitate the Master? We can also testify using the same Law to show sinners their personal transgressions. The next time you witness, use the Ten Commandments as Jesus did, and watch what happens.

There goes another minute.
Gone forever. Go share your faith
while you still have time.

Whoever Transgresses

When Jesus spoke to the woman at the well, in John chapter 4 He said that the Samaritans didn't know what they worshipped.[8] This is true of all the religions of the world. They are in ignorance as the true nature of the God who revealed Himself to Moses. Paul said this in Acts 17:23 when He said that the Athenians were in ignorance. We are even told in 1 Corinthians 10:20 that the Gentiles sacrifice to demons and not to God, while Scripture narrows it even further: "Whoever transgresses and does not abide in the doctrine of Christ does not have God."[9] That's why we must take them to Mount Sinai, let the thunder of the Law strip sinners of self-righteousness, and bring them to the foot of Calvary's cross. And how shall they hear without a preacher?

There goes another minute. *Gone forever.* **Go share your faith while you still have time.**

TICK ...
TICK ...
TICK ...
TICK ...
TICK ...
TICK ...
TICK ...
TICK ...
TICK ...
TICK ...
TICK ...
TICK ...
TICK ...
TICK ...
TICK ...
TICK ...
TICK ...
TICK ...
TICK ...
TICK ...
TICK ...
TICK ...
TICK ...
TICK ...
TICK ...
TICK ...

Like the Stars Forever

The Bible says that those who turn many to righteousness will shine like the stars forever.[10] If we are wise, we will want to turn many to the righteousness that's in Christ, because it is *righteousness* that delivers us from death. It saves us from God's terrible wrath. Jesus said, "Blessed are they who *thirst* for righteousness,"[11] but how can we help sin-loving sinners to thirst for righteousness? The answer is that we can use the Law to help them to see their sin in its true light. Remember that it's the Holy Spirit who reproves the world of sin, of *righteousness* and judgment to come.[12] Using the Law helps the world to understand that they *need* righteousness, because of the judgment to come. Without perfect righteousness, they will perish under God's wrath.

There goes another minute.
Gone forever. Go share your faith
while you still have time.

Witnessing to Telemarketers

When a telemarketer calls, let your little light shine … through the phone. When he says, "I have a real deal for you. It won't cost you a thing," ask for his name and then say, "It's good to hear from you. Have you been having a good day?" Listen to his reaction. Your genuine warmth will probably shock him. Then say, "May I ask you a few questions?" If he's been trained to be congenial, he will react positively. Then ask, "Do you consider yourself to be a good person?" If you mess up, say, "Gotta go. Thanks for calling." Then hang up. It's not hard. So, don't stay in the tomb of dead silence. Ask God to send His angels to roll the stone of fear away. Then come out of the tomb. It's not as hard as you may think, so be ready for your next telemarketer.

There goes another minute.
Gone forever. Go share your faith
while you still have time.

"You Can't Do This"

Being a witness of Jesus Christ is a mindset. If you haven't already done so, go to Gethsemane, drop to your knees, sweat great drops of blood at the thought of sharing your faith, and then say, "Not my will but Yours be done." That will give you the mindset to deny yourself and daily pick up the cross. You only have to bear the reproach of the cross for a short time. One day you will exchange it for a crown, and that day isn't too far away. So, if you have dealt with your fears, every time fear knocks at the door, you can send faith to answer it. When your cowardly cringing heart says, "You can't do this," you simply ignore its whispering and say, "I dealt with you at Gethsemane. Now I can do all things through Christ who strengthens me."

There goes another minute.
Gone forever. Go share your faith
while you still have time.

Applause at the Altar

The response to many altar calls isn't one of solemnity. Instead, there is often joy-filled applause. What's wrong with that? There is a problem. If the gospel has been preached biblically, i.e. sinners have been told that they have offended God by transgressing His Law, and they are responding in contrition, then it's a *solemn* assembly. Clapping then would be like a child who had lied to and stolen from his father, coming to him to apologize, and the mother bursting into applause. The timing would be inappropriate. Sure, there is joy in Heaven when one sinner repents, and only Heaven knows those who are genuinely repentant. So, it's wise to wait for fruit before we applaud, and in the meantime, keep seeking the lost.

There goes another minute. *Gone forever.* Go share your faith while you still have time.

TICK ...
TICK ...
TICK ...
TICK ...
TICK ...
TICK ...
TICK ...
TICK ...
TICK ...
TICK ...
TICK ...
TICK ...
TICK ...
TICK ...
TICK ...
TICK ...
TICK ...
TICK ...
TICK ...
TICK ...
TICK ...
TICK ...
TICK ...
TICK ...
TICK ...
TICK ...
TICK ...

The Mind of God

Do you ever think about how God sees the thought-life of every single human being on the face of this earth? But He is not confined to those that are living. He isn't confined to time. He also sees the thought-life of every single person who has ever lived from the beginning to the last minute of all time. He sees the Russians who think in the Russian language, and He hears every tribe of every nation in their native languages. He knows how many hairs are upon the head of each and every person. He's also intimately familiar with the inside of a pebble hidden a thousand miles into the soil of the planet Mars. He made it, so He knows what's in it. How incredible God is. And this same God commands us to preach His Gospel to every creature, and even promises to go with us.

There goes another minute.
Gone forever. Go share your faith
while you still have time.

TICK ...
TICK ...
TICK ...
TICK ...
TICK ...
TICK ...
TICK ...
TICK ...
TICK ...
TICK ...
TICK ...
TICK ...
TICK ...
TICK ...
TICK ...
TICK ...
TICK ...
TICK ...
TICK ...
TICK ...
TICK ...
TICK ...
TICK ...
TICK ...
TICK ...
TICK ...
TICK ...

To Be a Soul-winner

It seems that God has a special smile for those who throw themselves into the task of seeking to save the lost. In John chapter four, when Jesus told His disciples that He ate something of which they knew nothing, He had been sharing the Gospel. The great Bible commentator, Matthew Henry, said, "I would think it a greater happiness to gain one soul to Christ than mountains of silver and gold to myself." Charles Spurgeon said, "To be a soul winner is the happiest thing in this world." While we can obtain pleasure from reading the Bible, from fellowship with other Christians, and from worship, seeking the lost (and doing it biblically) gives the Christian a unique satisfaction. Philemon 1:6 says that if you share your faith, it will open up a deeper spiritual realm. Dive into that deeper realm today.

There goes another minute.
Gone forever. Go share your faith
while you still have time.

Think of the Sun

Think of the greatness of the sun. It silently rises and sets each day, painting our skies with magnificent colors. Yet every second, millions of tons of hydrogen are destroyed in explosions that start somewhere near the core of our sun, where the temperature is 13 million degrees Celsius. That's *hot*. The earth's entire oil, coal and wood reserves would fuel its energy output to the earth alone for only a few days. Tongues of hydrogen flame leap from the surface with the force of 1,000 million hydrogen bombs! They are thrust up by the enormous thermonuclear explosion at the core of the sun where 564 million tons of hydrogen fuse each second to form helium. Almighty God created it, and guilty sinners have to face Him on the Day of His Wrath. What an unspeakably fearful thing.

There goes another minute.
Gone forever. Go share your faith
while you still have time.

TICK ...
TICK ...
TICK ...
TICK ...
TICK ...
TICK ...
TICK ...
TICK ...
TICK ...
TICK ...
TICK ...
TICK ...
TICK ...
TICK ...
TICK ...
TICK ...
TICK ...
TICK ...
TICK ...
TICK ...
TICK ...
TICK ...
TICK ...
TICK ...
TICK ...
TICK ...

59

Eternity on the Eyes

Do you realize that God's Law is the unmovable rock that will forever stop the flow of the *River Life* for every human being who dies in his sins? It will damn them forever! What a terrifying horror: to be damned for eternity! Yet, so few are warned. So, shake of any thoughts of tickling ears with carefully chosen words that don't offend, and do what Jesus did. Speak the truth in love. Keep their fate before your mind. Inscribe "eternity" on your eyes. Our time is so limited. This life is like a dry and burning desert. Time is like precious water cupped in your hands. Only an ignorant person will let its life-giving drops fall through his or her fingers. Benjamin Franklin said, "Do you love life? Then do not squander time, for that is the stuff life is made of."

There goes another minute.
Gone forever. Go share your faith
while you still have time.

Icy Tribulation

Trials bring us to our knees to seek God's will rather than our own. In South Korea, a baseball team began a training program with a difference. They would climb a high mountain, remove their shirts, and stand bare-chested in the freezing wind. Then they would dig holes in the ice, and subject their bodies to freezing cold water. They said that the practice made them hardy, and also promoted team unity. Their team went from being a laughingstock to the top of the league. As much as we don't like the thought, blessings tend to take our eyes off God. Trials put them back on. Icy tribulation builds strength of character within the Christian, and the cold winds of persecution purify us and bring a sense of unity and purpose. And that purpose is to seek the lost.

There goes another minute.
Gone forever. Go share your faith
while you still have time.

TICK ...

Kick For Dear Life

TICK ...

Muscle grows through resistance. If you
want to grow physically, get into a
swimming pool and hold a five-gallon
container filled with water at head level.
To stay afloat, you will have to kick for
dear life. The key in this exercise is to
have the lid off the container, face it
down and let the water drain out as you
kick. A great consolation is that you
know that as time passes, as you become
tired, the weight is going to get lighter,
and that knowledge will spur you on. As
you step into the waters of personal
evangelism, the weight of apprehension
may seem unbearable at first, but as you
pour yourself out for the Gospel, you
will have the knowledge that God will
relieve you of the weight. Each time you
exercise yourself in this, you will
strengthen yourself spiritually.

There goes another minute.
Gone forever. Go share your faith
while you still have time.

The Ledge of Futility

When firemen saw the man on the ledge of the twelfth floor, smoke was billowing out from the structure, blinding the terrified man, and forcing him to the very edge. Quickly, a fireman was lowered from above by a rope, and rescued him. The man said that it was a miracle that he was saved. He said that he was blinded by smoke, but heard the voice of his rescuer, and from there, clung to him for dear life. We once stood on ledge of futility. We stood blind, fearful, helpless, and hopeless... *until we heard the voice of our Savior.* He reached down from the heavens with His holy hand and snatched us from death's dark door. *But there are still others on the ledge going through the terror we once experienced.* We cannot rest until we direct them into the hands of Jesus.

There goes another minute.
Gone forever. Go share your faith
while you still have time.

TICK ...
TICK ...
TICK ...
TICK ...
TICK ...
TICK ...
TICK ...
TICK ...
TICK ...
TICK ...
TICK ...
TICK ...
TICK ...
TICK ...
TICK ...
TICK ...
TICK ...
TICK ...
TICK ...
TICK ...
TICK ...
TICK ...
TICK ...
TICK ...
TICK ...
TICK ...

63

The Alarm of Conscience

The moment we are saved, we find that the world, the flesh and the devil plague us. The appetite of the flesh was once satisfied with the pleasures of sin, but upon conversion, it is starved and begins to gnaw at the mind for want of food. It causes what the Scriptures call a "war in [our] members."[13] Thoughts, which once were acceptable, suddenly stir the alarm of conscience, and that alarm of conscience is there as a warning of the fires of Hell. It's a smoke detector that alarms us because we are new creatures in Christ Jesus. Old things have passed away, and all things have become new. The old sinful nature, like four-days-dead Lazarus, now stinks because it is dead in Christ. So, bury it, and live to do the will of the God who called you out of darkness into light.

There goes another minute.
Gone forever. Go share your faith
while you still have time.

Going Back to Sin

Are you filled with an inexpressible gratitude for the "unspeakable gift" of the Cross? Have you seen Jesus Christ "evidently set forth and crucified?" Can you say with Paul, "God forbid that I should glory, save in the Cross of our Lord Jesus Christ, by whom the world is crucified to me, and I to the world"[14]? After seeing the love of the cross, how could we ever go back to the pleasures of sin? To do so, we have to trample underfoot the blood of Jesus Christ. We would have to count the sacrifice of Calvary as nothing. Instead, we willfully crucify ourselves to the world. We whisper with the hymnist, "When I survey the wondrous cross, on which the Prince of Glory died, my richest gain I count but loss, and pour contempt on all my pride."

**There goes another minute.
Gone forever. Go share your faith
while you still have time.**

TICK ...
TICK ...
TICK ...
TICK ...
TICK ...
TICK ...
TICK ...
TICK ...
TICK ...
TICK ...
TICK ...
TICK ...
TICK ...
TICK ...
TICK ...
TICK ...
TICK ...
TICK ...
TICK ...
TICK ...
TICK ...
TICK ...
TICK ...
TICK ...
TICK ...
TICK ...

65

Deliberate Resistance

The army that doesn't train well will not fight well. Soldiers are not only trained in the use of their weapons, but deliberate resistance is put in front of every soldier. He finds himself facing obstacle courses. He weaves his way through all types of difficulties, bunkers, hazards, hindrances, snags, tripwires, hurdles, hedges, and barriers. He is made to run with great weights upon his shoulders, march for miles, arise at the crack of dawn, and stand for long periods of time. He is forced to go against the grain. The objective is to create a strong, disciplined, finely tuned, well regulated, and organized force of soldiers who will stop at nothing to achieve the objective. Wimps drop out, and we drop out the moment we forget the cause for which we fight—to seek and save the lost.

There goes another minute.
Gone forever. Go share your faith
while you still have time.

Rippling Muscles

The strong, muscular, conquering hero didn't get that way through easy living. To attain such a physical state, he had to train hard. Through many years of running, weight training, and self-discipline, he brought himself to the peak of condition. The more resistance he put against his muscles, the more they developed. God wants to bring each of us to the peak of condition. He is refining us through resistance. He desires to build in us the muscles of a strong and good character. He doesn't want us to be caught up in the vanities of this futile life. He wants to teach us good judgment, self-discipline, perseverance, godliness, and love. These are the rippling muscles that impress God. So, flex your muscle today by lifting up the cross of Calvary in front of this dying world. Seek and save the lost.

There goes another minute.
Gone forever. **Go share your faith**
while you still have time.

The God-conscience Part

Sinners walk around on God's earth, breathing God's air and seeing God's flowers, His birds, His trees, His sun— and yet they not aware of Him. There's a reason for this. It's because they are spiritually dead. The world is like an appliance with the plug pulled out. We are made up of three main parts: body, soul, and spirit. The body is the machine we walk around in. It is fearfully and wonderfully made. The soul is the self-conscious part—the area of the emotions, the will, and the conscience. But the spirit is our *God*-conscious part. If people are not aware of God, it is because their receivers are dead. They are, as the Bible says "without understanding." Yet from the moment they are plugged in through the new birth, they become aware that "in Him we live and move and have our being."

There goes another minute. *Gone forever*. Go share your faith while you still have time.

TICK ...
TICK ...
TICK ...
TICK ...
TICK ...
TICK ...
TICK ...
TICK ...
TICK ...
TICK ...
TICK ...
TICK ...
TICK ...
TICK ...
TICK ...
TICK ...
TICK ...
TICK ...
TICK ...
TICK ...
TICK ...
TICK ...
TICK ...
TICK ...
TICK ...
TICK ...

Study to Share

The Apostle Paul said, "Study to show yourself approved to God, a workman that *needs not to be ashamed* … " We need never be ashamed. The key is to "*Study* to show yourself approved to God." *Study* how to share your faith. It's as simple as that. We should study the subject. A great preacher once said, "It is the great business of every Christian to save souls. People complain that they do not know how to take hold of this matter. Why, the reason is plain enough; *they have never studied it.* They have never taken the proper pains to qualify themselves for the work. *If you do not make it a matter of study,* how you may successfully act in building up the kingdom of Christ, you are acting a very wicked and absurd part as a Christian."

There goes another minute.
Gone forever. **Go share your faith while you still have time.**

TICK ...
TICK ...
TICK ...
TICK ...
TICK ...
TICK ...
TICK ...
TICK ...
TICK ...
TICK ...
TICK ...
TICK ...
TICK ...
TICK ...
TICK ...
TICK ...
TICK ...
TICK ...
TICK ...
TICK ...
TICK ...
TICK ...
TICK ...
TICK ...
TICK ...
TICK ...
TICK ...
TICK ...

69

There is No Fear of God

Listen to the Apostle Paul in the Book of Acts, as he preaches the Gospel: "Men of Israel, *and you that fear God*, give audience."[15] His message was for the men of Israel and for *those who feared God*. The psalmist says a similar thing, "Come and hear, *all you that fear God*, and I will declare what he has done for my soul."[16] There's a reason why the Gospel is for those who fear God: "By mercy and truth iniquity is purged: *and by the fear of the Lord men depart from evil*."[17] The problem is that sinful men *don't* fear God. The Bible tells us, "There is no fear of God before their eyes."[18] So, with God's help, we have to put it there, and we do that by preaching The Ten Commandments and future punishment, as Jesus did.

There goes another minute.
Gone forever. Go share your faith
while you still have time.

Never Caught Off Guard

Do you ever think about the greatness of God? He is omniscient. That means He knows everything. He never suddenly thinks of something. If God did suddenly think of something that He had never thought of before, then He wouldn't be omniscient. He is also omnipresent. He dwells everywhere. If you travel 100 billion miles into space *in any direction,* God is there. He's also omnipotent. That means He can do anything. All this means that He's never caught off guard or says "Oops!" He never makes a mistake. How unspeakably great is our God. What a fearful thing it will be to stand before Him on Judgment Day. But that's what sinners will do. And this same God commands us to preach His forgiveness to every creature. And when we go into the world to preach, He's already there, waiting to help us.

There goes another minute.
Gone forever. **Go share your faith while you still have time.**

Giant Despair

In *Pilgrim's Progress*, Christian and Faithful found themselves in Doubting Castle, being tormented by Giant Despair. However, they discovered a way out of that dungeon when Faithful put his hand into his breast and found the "Key of Promise." Put the promises of God into your heart, and every time Giant Despair tries to lock you in his dirty dungeon of despair, grab hold of that liberating key. God's promises are supernatural. So, memorize them and then speak them out loud to the enemy. That's what Jesus did when the devil whispered suicidal thoughts to Him, and when he tried to seduce Him into Satan worship. The Bible says "Submit to God. Resist the devil and he *will* flee from you." The key is to be submitted to God. If you are submitted to Him, you will obey The Great Commission and preach the Gospel to every creator.

There goes another minute.
Gone forever. **Go share your faith while you still have time.**

Christian Youth

Back in 2002, a report revealed that 76 percent of American secular youth admitted to cheating on a test, 85 percent had lied to a teacher, and 93 percent had lied to a parent. The alarming thing about the report was that there was little or no difference between these statistics and statistics among professing "Christian Youth." The results confirm the suspicion that our churches are filled with people who are not saved. How we must pray for our churches, and see them as mission fields. We need to pray for our pastors—that they will see themselves as missionaries, open up the Ten Commandments as Jesus did, and thunder their decrees from the pulpit. History teaches us that this is how to awaken a generation to the reality of the cross, and their need of repentance and faith in Jesus.

There goes another minute.
Gone forever. Go share your faith
while you still have time.

TICK ...
TICK ...
TICK ...
TICK ...
TICK ...
TICK ...
TICK ...
TICK ...
TICK ...
TICK ...
TICK ...
TICK ...
TICK ...
TICK ...
TICK ...
TICK ...
TICK ...
TICK ...
TICK ...
TICK ...
TICK ...
TICK ...
TICK ...
TICK ...
TICK ...
TICK ...

73

What Advantage Has the Jew

The Book of Romans asks if the Jew has any advantage over the Gentile. The answer is "Much every way: chiefly, because that to them were committed the oracles of God."[19] The words, "oracles of God," are obvious reference to the Moral Law. Any Jew who has knowledge of the Law has the advantage of knowing the nature of sin. He knows the standards of God. He sees sin as being exceedingly sinful. The Book of Hebrews also makes reference to "the oracles of God"— "For when for the time you ought to be teachers, you have need that one teach you again which be the first principles of the oracles of God..."[20] The Moral Law is a foundation upon which "sound doctrine" stands. We ought to be teachers, and we ought to be teaching the Law to sinners. That will show them that they need a Savior.

There goes another minute.
Gone forever. **Go share your faith while you still have time.**

Feeding Your Zeal

Experience has shown that those, who know what they have been saved *from*, know what they have been saved *for*. If you realize that you are a terrible sinner, worthy of Hell, and you know that you have been saved from such a terrible place, you will seek to see others saved also. It is the Moral Law that reveals that sin is exceedingly sinful, and therefore it makes grace abound in the hearts of those who come to Christ. If this is your experience, you find that gratitude for God's mercy continually feeds your zeal to do His will, and you will want to bring others through the same door. Each of us must understand that it is the Law of God that prepares the way for the Gospel to do its work. It is the solid soil from which Calvary's Cross arises. This is the foundation for biblical evangelism.

**There goes another minute.
Gone forever. Go share your faith
while you still have time.**

TICK ...
TICK ...
TICK ...
TICK ...
TICK ...
TICK ...
TICK ...
TICK ...
TICK ...
TICK ...
TICK ...
TICK ...
TICK ...
TICK ...
TICK ...
TICK ...
TICK ...
TICK ...
TICK ...
TICK ...
TICK ...
TICK ...
TICK ...
TICK ...
TICK ...
TICK ...
TICK ...

Praying For Laborers

In Luke 10:2 Jesus said, "The harvest truly is great, but the laborers are few: pray therefore the Lord of the harvest, that he would send forth laborers into his harvest." It has been 2000 years since Jesus told His disciples to seek God in prayer for laborers, and it seems that we still have the same dilemma. Bill Bright said, "Only two percent of believers in America regularly share their faith in Christ with others."[21] One would therefore suspect that Luke 10:2 is probably the most neglected exhortation to prayer in the Bible. Who is going to feel comfortable praying for laborers if he is not laboring in the harvest fields himself? Change that today. Pray for laborers and then say, "Here I am Lord; send me," and then obey The Great Commission to go into all the world and preach the Gospel to every creature.

**There goes another minute.
Gone forever. Go share your faith
while you still have time.**

We Will Stay and Pray

Are you praying for revival? Many are. They aren't seeking the lost. They instead see revival as a *sovereign* "move of God." In doing so, they are handing the job of evangelism back to Heaven. In essence they are saying, "We know you have commanded us to preach the Gospel to every creature ... but we will stay here and pray. Your Word says, 'How will they hear without a preacher?' ... but we will stay here and pray. You have told us that the *Gospel* is the power of God to salvation ... but we will stay here and pray because it sure is easier *to talk to God about men, rather than to talk to men about God.*" Don't be like that. If we love Him, we will keep His commandments, and one of His commandments is go into all the world and preach the Gospel to every creature.

There goes another minute.
Gone forever. Go share your faith
while you still have time.

Lord, Lord

TICK ...
TICK ...
TICK ...
TICK ...
TICK ...
TICK ...
TICK ...
TICK ...
TICK ...
TICK ...
TICK ...
TICK ...
TICK ...
TICK ...
TICK ...
TICK ...
TICK ...
TICK ...
TICK ...
TICK ...
TICK ...
TICK ...
TICK ...
TICK ...
TICK ...
TICK ...
TICK ...

Those who don't share their faith need to be reminded of the sobering warnings of Jesus that on the Day of Judgment many will cry, "Lord, Lord," but will hear, "Depart from Me ... I never knew you." The Bible says that the lukewarm will be spewed out of the mouth of Christ. These verses should make all tremble in fear those who name the name of Christ, yet lack concern for the unsaved. Some are false converts and need to be awakened by the Law; others are Christians who have not been taught the biblical priory of the Church—that they have a moral responsibility to reach out to the lost. There are masses within the Body of Christ who have never once identified with Paul's "Woe unto me if I preach not the Gospel," and as long as they remain in that state, we will lack laborers.

**There goes another minute.
Gone forever. Go share your faith
while you still have time.**

Human Confrontation

God has saved multitudes through Gospel tracts, so always carry them with you, and take a moment to encourage other Christians to do the same. Let them know that Christian literature can be used as a conversation opener. One of the most difficult things about witnessing is starting a conversation about God. A tract can do that for you. It can be left with the person you have spoken to, so that he or she can read further about the way of salvation. Tracts can be given to people when it's not convenient to speak to them. Simply say, "Did you get one of these?" If you find that difficult, you could at least leave them in places without the daunting thought of human confrontation. Whatever you do, never let a day go by when you don't do *something* to reach the lost while you still can.

There goes another minute.
Gone forever. **Go share your faith while you still have time.**

TICK ...
TICK ...
TICK ...
TICK ...
TICK ...
TICK ...
TICK ...
TICK ...
TICK ...
TICK ...
TICK ...
TICK ...
TICK ...
TICK ...
TICK ...
TICK ...
TICK ...
TICK ...
TICK ...
TICK ...
TICK ...
TICK ...
TICK ...
TICK ...
TICK ...
TICK ...
TICK ...

The Vow of Silence

We may shake our heads when we think of the oxymoron of monks with a lifetime vow of silence. They profess to know God, but never preach the Gospel to the unsaved. They are dead to the world. Many in the Church are like that. Like four days dead Lazarus, they have nothing to do with the outside world. They have been scared to death by the very thought of "evangelism." They sit paralyzed on the pew, wrapped in the shroud of the fear of man. Therefore, we must groan in prayer for them, and like Jesus outside the tomb of Lazarus, lift up our voices and call the dead Church to come out of the grave. There is great joy among laborers when a cold and lifeless corpse comes out of the tomb of inactivity to be a living witness of Him Who is the resurrection and the life.

There goes another minute.
Gone forever. Go share your faith
while you still have time.

80

Our Moral State

Romans chapter three gives a stinging indictment of the moral state of humanity. It says that we are corrupt, ignorant, rebellious, and violent. Then it gives the cause of such a sinful state: "There is no fear of God before their eyes," and immediately swings the subject to God's Law ... the cure for the moral dilemma. Psalm 111:10 says, "The fear of the Lord is the beginning of wisdom: a good understanding have all they that do his commandments." Therefore, *preach* that which is the beginning of wisdom. Teach the true character of our Creator, using the Law to show His perfect righteousness. This is what God has used throughout history to bring about true revival. This is what He uses to awaken a lost and dying world. This is what Jesus did to show sinners that they needed a savior. Make sure you imitate Him.

There goes another minute.
Gone forever. **Go share your faith while you still have time.**

TICK ...
TICK ...
TICK ...
TICK ...
TICK ...
TICK ...
TICK ...
TICK ...
TICK ...
TICK ...
TICK ...
TICK ...
TICK ...
TICK ...
TICK ...
TICK ...
TICK ...
TICK ...
TICK ...
TICK ...
TICK ...
TICK ...
TICK ...
TICK ...
TICK ...
TICK ...
TICK ...

81

Enemies of God

Few nowadays hear preaching that shows that sinners are enemies of God in their minds through wicked works. Most don't know that they are children of wrath by nature. They don't realize that God's wrath "abides" on them. The Bible tells us that our God is a consuming fire, and it is a fearful thing to fall into His holy hands. Eyes should be plucked out, and hands severed at the thought of sinning against Him. We should fear Him who has power to cast the body and soul into Hell. It is when we see Him in truth that we will say with Paul, "Wherefore knowing the terror of the Lord, we persuade men."[22] Those, who don't persuade men, don't know the terror of the Lord. So, open up the Ten Commandments, let His terror be known, and watch how it persuades men.

There goes another minute.
Gone forever. Go share your faith
while you still have time.

A Good Understanding

After speaking of the fear of the Lord, Psalm 111 says, "A good understanding have all they that do his commandments." It is the Commandments that make sinners and saints tremble. The Law puts the fear of God in our hearts. Sinners tremble when they have an understanding that the wrath of the Law calls for their blood. Saints tremble at the foot of a bloodied cross, because it was the Law that called for their blood, but instead shed the precious blood of the Savior. The Bible tells us that it is the fear of the Lord that makes men depart from sin both before and after the Cross. It doesn't disappear when we come to know His love. It continues to do its most necessary work: "The fear of the Lord tends to life: and he that has it shall abide satisfied; he shall not be visited with evil."[23]

There goes another minute.
Gone forever. Go share your faith
while you still have time.

TICK ...
TICK ...
TICK ...
TICK ...
TICK ...
TICK ...
TICK ...
TICK ...
TICK ...
TICK ...
TICK ...
TICK ...
TICK ...
TICK ...
TICK ...
TICK ...
TICK ...
TICK ...
TICK ...
TICK ...
TICK ...
TICK ...
TICK ...
TICK ...
TICK ...
TICK ...

Pulling Sinners From the Fire

Scripture likens sin to leprosy, a disease characterized by spots on the flesh. A symptom of leprosy is that the victim loses any sense of pain. Mild pain makes us move around when we sit down for too long in one position. This allows blood to freely flow throughout our body, and our blood is the life of our flesh. If there is no pain, there is no movement, and as a consequence, the flesh rots. Sin dulls the pains of an accusing conscience, so that there is no movement from it, i.e. no repentance. It causes "fleshly lusts, which *war* against the soul."[24] Remember that Jesus is coming for a spotless Church—for a "glorious church, without spot or wrinkle," so keep yourself "*unspotted* from the world." And make sure you pull sinners from the fire, hating "even the garment *spotted* by the flesh."[25]

There goes another minute. *Gone forever*. Go share your faith while you still have time.

Speaking of Wrath

It's not enough to preach the Ten Commandments, or even to open up the spiritual nature of the Law. We must also preach Judgment Day and of the reality of Hell. Without the threat of punishment, no one will flee from the wrath that is to come. The thought of the existence of Hell will be scorned if the Law *and the consequences of its transgression* are not preached. Great damage has been done for the cause of the Gospel by "Hell-fire" preaching— that is the preaching of Hell without the "reasoning" of the Law. But great damage has also been done by swinging the pendulum too far the other way, and never talking about these terrible realities. A failure to speak of God's wrath not only leaves sinners with the delusion that God isn't to be feared, but it also defuses evangelism of any sense of urgency.

There goes another minute.
Gone forever. **Go share your faith while you still have time.**

TICK ...
TICK ...
TICK ...
TICK ...
TICK ...
TICK ...
TICK ...
TICK ...
TICK ...
TICK ...
TICK ...
TICK ...
TICK ...
TICK ...
TICK ...
TICK ...
TICK ...
TICK ...
TICK ...
TICK ...
TICK ...
TICK ...
TICK ...
TICK ...
TICK ...

The Holy Huddle

Many Christians live in monasteries without walls. They fellowship in the holy huddle and cozy comfort of the Saved. Excommunicate yourself from the monastery. We are called to be *in*, but not *of* the world: "That you may be blameless and harmless, the sons of God, without rebuke, in the midst of a crooked and perverse nation, among whom you shine as lights in the world."[26] We should be *in the midst, among whom, in the world.* We should be accused (like Jesus) of being a friend of sinners, and our mingling with them should be motivated by a deep concern for their eternal welfare. This is something that you will have to make yourself do if you want to do what God tells you to do. He proved His love for you by dying on the cross. Now you prove your love for Him by taking that cross to a dying world.

There goes another minute.
Gone forever. Go share your faith
while you still have time.

Fervent Heat

Have you ever heard a clap of thunder that was so loud it seemed to make the heavens tremble? It will be but a tiny whisper compared to the "great noise" and "flaming fire" that will be revealed when Almighty God rips apart the sky at the Second Coming. In that "great and terrible Day of the Lord," the elements "shall melt with fervent heat, the earth also and the works that are therein shall be burned up."[27] Is there any fear when we read these words: "Whose voice then shook the earth: but now he has promised, saying, Yet once more I shake not the earth only, but also Heaven"[28]? Where is our horror at the fate of the lost? How can we not care that the unsaved are pouring into Hell like sheep being run over a great cliff? Apparently, we must be the most hard-hearted generation since Adam.

There goes another minute. *Gone forever*. Go share your faith while you still have time.

Love and Faith

In the Epistle of Paul to Philemon, he says that he has heard of the "love and faith" which he has toward both the Lord and his brethren. Then he says that the "sharing of your faith may become effective by the acknowledgement of every good thing which is in you in Christ Jesus."[29] The Greek word for "effective" means "active, operative and powerful." Isn't that what we want? We want to be active, operative, and powerful in our witness for the Gospel. The key to getting this is clear. Both the love and faith Paul spoke of are not passive. They must have *action*. If we have love for God and man, we will share our faith, because from love and faith spring the fruits of the Spirit. Love will produce goodness, gentleness, and patience, while faith issues joy and peace.

There goes another minute. *Gone forever*. Go share your faith while you still have time.

Dry Eyes, Hard Heart

Few of us have to be reminded of the love of God in Christ. But that cross should also speak of the wrath of God and the fate of the ungodly. We must pray for tender hearts that will weigh heavy if we meet an unsaved person, or even walk past them without reaching out either in words or with the written word. May our evident, tender hearts shame the hard hearts within the Church. It seems that most of us can weep at every human tragedy, and even the death of a pet dog, but we never even shed a tear at the ultimate tragedy of Hell. Our dry eyes reveal hard hearts. We either don't believe the horror that "whosoever was not found written in the book of life was cast into the lake of fire" (Revelation 20:15), or we don't care. Both are sin.

There goes another minute.
Gone forever. **Go share your faith while you still have time.**

TICK ...
TICK ...
TICK ...
TICK ...
TICK ...
TICK ...
TICK ...
TICK ...
TICK ...
TICK ...
TICK ...
TICK ...
TICK ...
TICK ...
TICK ...
TICK ...
TICK ...
TICK ...
TICK ...
TICK ...
TICK ...
TICK ...
TICK ...
TICK ...
TICK ...
TICK ...
TICK ...

89

Consider the President

Consider the late President Kennedy. One moment he was sitting in his limo with his wife, smiling and waving to adoring crowds. The next moment he was in eternity. A small piece of fast-moving metal sent him there in a split second. Imagine you were taken back to the time just before he stepped into the limo. You can't stop the assassination, but you can talk to him for a few moments about his eternal salvation. Are you so intimidated by his status that you would remain silent? Of course not! You know what will happen to him. You look beyond the presidency into eternity. You ignore your fears and look into his eyes. You see the frailty of his humanity, and think how in an instant of time he will be blasted into death. Now think of the rest of humanity ... death will take 150,000 into eternity in the next 24 hours.

There goes another minute.
Gone forever. Go share your faith
while you still have time.

The Oracles of God

The Bible says "If any man speak, let him speak as the oracles of God … " What does it mean: "as the oracles of God?". Notice it says, "oracles," not "oracle." What specifically are the "oracles of God?" Stephen tells us in Acts 7:38. He says, "This is he, that was in the church in the wilderness with the angel which spoke to him in the mount Sinai, and with our fathers: who received the lively oracles to give to us." He says that the oracles were given to Moses on Mount Sinai. The "oracles of God" is a specific reference to the Moral Law. So, if you are going to speak for the Lord, make sure you are speak as the oracles of God. Do what Jesus did—open up the Ten Commandments and show sinners how they need a Savior. And do it today.

There goes another minute.
Gone forever. Go share your faith
while you still have time.

TICK ...
TICK ...
TICK ...
TICK ...
TICK ...
TICK ...
TICK ...
TICK ...
TICK ...
TICK ...
TICK ...
TICK ...
TICK ...
TICK ...
TICK ...
TICK ...
TICK ...
TICK ...
TICK ...
TICK ...
TICK ...
TICK ...
TICK ...
TICK ...
TICK ...
TICK ...
TICK ...
TICK ...

91

He Must Be Fined

Millions are unsaved because they think that all that is necessary to get right with God is to ask for His forgiveness. To counter this, use the following illustration: A criminal is standing before a good judge in a court of law, guilty of a terrible crime for which there is a $50,000 fine. If he simply says, "Judge, I know I'm guilty of this serious crime, but I'm truly sorry and I won't do it again," is the judge going to then let him go? Of course not. He *should* be sorry for what he's done, and of course, he shouldn't do it again. The judge is bound by the law. He *must* fine him. He must make sure that justice is done or the judge himself is corrupt. So, open up God's Law to show sinners that they are condemned, and the cross is their only hope of salvation.

**There goes another minute.
Gone forever. Go share your faith
while you still have time.**

I Thought You Might Like This

Do you ever buy food for unsaved people? It can speak volumes to a hardened sinner. We are told in Scripture, "For this is the will of God, that by doing good you may put to silence the ignorance of foolish men."[30] So, if you find that someone is always arguing with you, put him to silence by buying something delicious for him. Then leave it where he will find it, along with a tasteful card. Don't write anything "religious" on the card. Simply say, "I saw this and thought that you might like it." Don't give him anything to argue with. Then pray that your small expression of love will soften his hard heart, so that you can speak to him about the *big* expression of love revealed in the cross. Don't put this off for another day. It may never come.

**There goes another minute.
Gone forever. Go share your faith
while you still have time.**

TICK ...
TICK ...
TICK ...
TICK ...
TICK ...
TICK ...
TICK ...
TICK ...
TICK ...
TICK ...
TICK ...
TICK ...
TICK ...
TICK ...
TICK ...
TICK ...
TICK ...
TICK ...
TICK ...
TICK ...
TICK ...
TICK ...
TICK ...
TICK ...
TICK ...
TICK ...
TICK ...
TICK ...

93

You Know What Awaits

All around us, people are concerned with things that don't matter in the light of eternity. They are more concerned with what they will have for dinner than they are about where they will spend eternity. God isn't in their thoughts. They have no concept of the eternal. But you do. You know what awaits them. So, take the initiative. Look into eternity. This is the spirit of, "We do not look at the things which are seen, but at the things which are not seen. For the things which are seen are temporary; but the things which are not seen are eternal."[31] Commit your way to our immortal and invisible Creator, and then watch Him faithfully direct your paths. Plead with Him for divine encounters—people that He supernaturally puts into your path. Do this, and do it today.

There goes another minute.
Gone forever. **Go share your faith while you still have time.**

The Helper in the Sky

The Bible tells us that eternal life is the free gift of God. It cannot be earned. Those who think that they can merit salvation are in a delusion about God. They see Him as their friend, the Helper in the sky upon whom they can call when they have problems. However, the Bible teaches us the opposite. It tells us that God is not our friend, and that He's actually our enemy. It also tells us that if we come to Him with a proud heart, He will resist us. It even says that our sins have made a separation between God and us so that He won't even hear our prayers. Such thoughts are offensive to a godless world, but they are the truth. They will never truly repent as long as they don't know the truth. God has given us another day to speak the truth in love.

There goes another minute.
Gone forever. Go share your faith
while you still have time.

A Prison Into a Palace

Listen to George Whitefield encourage an open air preacher: "Let the love of Jesus constrain you to go out into the highways and hedges to compel poor sinners to come in. Some may say, 'This is not proceeding with a zeal according to knowledge;' but I am persuaded ... the Gospel must be propagated in the same manner as it was first established, by itinerant preaching. Go on, dear sir, go on and follow your glorious Master without the camp, bearing His reproach. Never fear the scourge of the tongue, or the threatenings that are daily breathed out against the Lord, and against His Christ. Suffer we must. Perhaps, we may sing in a prison, and have our feet in the stocks; but faith in Jesus turns a prison into a palace, and makes a bed of flames become a bed of [feathers]."

There goes another minute.
Gone forever. **Go share your faith while you still have time.**

TICK ... TICK ...

Why Roses Have Thorns

Why do roses have thorns? They are so beautiful, and yet can be so painful. Perhaps it's to remind us of the beauty of the Garden of Eden that was marred by the curse of sin. Or perhaps God looked down through time and saw a suffering Savior, wearing a crown of thorns, and the sharp thorns on the rose stem are to remind us that you cannot have a Jesus without that crown of thorns. The world embraces a baby in a manger or a great teacher who espouses profound thought. They admire the beautiful rose and inhale the fragrant perfume, but there is no Jesus without the cross. There is no Rose of Sharon without the cruel crown. Anything else is what the Bible calls, "another Jesus." The Apostle Paul said that he gloried only in "Christ crucified," and we must do the same.

**There goes another minute.
Gone forever. Go share your faith
while you still have time.**

TICK ...
TICK ...
TICK ...
TICK ...
TICK ...
TICK ...
TICK ...
TICK ...
TICK ...
TICK ...
TICK ...
TICK ...
TICK ...
TICK ...
TICK ...
TICK ...
TICK ...
TICK ...
TICK ...
TICK ...
TICK ...
TICK ...
TICK ...
TICK ...
TICK ...
TICK ...
TICK ...
TICK ...
TICK ...
TICK ...
TICK ...

Mountains Out of Molehills

Do you ever feel afraid to approach a stranger and talk to him about the things of God? Does a little old lady suddenly look like Goliath when you go to pass her a Gospel tract? Imagine for a moment that you are not a Christian, and that some Christian is standing in the shadows, trembling in fear at the thought of giving *you* a Gospel tract. How would that make you feel? Wouldn't his fear be an insult to you as a person? What are you, some sort of monster? Of course not. So, treat others, as you would have them treat you. Don't make monsters out of molehills. Push aside your fears, say a warm, "Hello," and when the person answers you back, ask, "Did you get one of these?" and hand him or her a tract. If you will do that, you will find that your initial fears are unfounded.

**There goes another minute.
Gone forever. Go share your faith
while you still have time.**

The Evolutionists

There's a primitive tribe of people on this earth that need to hear the gospel. This is because they draw back from the truth, and choose to live in the jungles of spiritual darkness, bonded together in ignorant devil worship. Be warned: If you become a missionary and take the gospel to them, they might eat you alive. They speak a strange dialect of their own, but if we care, we have to learn to speak their language. We mustn't forget that (despite their strange and ignorant beliefs), these are human beings— made in the image of God. This is hard to believe, but they think that they came from apes. *Really.* They are called "The Evolutionists," and the only effective way to reach them is to use the Law as a schoolmaster to bring them to Christ.

There goes another minute.
Gone forever. Go share your faith
while you still have time.

TICK ...
TICK ...
TICK ...
TICK ...
TICK ...
TICK ...
TICK ...
TICK ...
TICK ...
TICK ...
TICK ...
TICK ...
TICK ...
TICK ...
TICK ...
TICK ...
TICK ...
TICK ...
TICK ...
TICK ...
TICK ...
TICK ...
TICK ...
TICK ...
TICK ...
TICK ...

Cozy Comfort

Have you ever seen an eagle's nest? It's way up there—a thousand feet up on the edge of a cliff, and the mother eagle is saying to her poor chick, "Get out and fly." He's terrified, and that's understandable because he's never done it before. He prefers the cozy comfort and safety of his mother's nest. So, she subtly takes all the feathers from the lining of the nest, leaving bare sticks to prod the chick, making it uncomfortable for him. Now he prefers to get out of the nest and stretch his wings. Does your conscience prick you and make you feel uncomfortable when we talk about your evangelistic responsibility? Maybe you never want to be involved in the irksome task of evangelism, but each of us must let such talk do so, and drive us out of the nest of complacency.

**There goes another minute.
Gone forever. Go share your faith
while you still have time.**

Pestilent Fellow

The Holy Spirit warned the Apostle Paul that bonds and afflictions awaited him wherever he went as a Christian. And they did. He was persecuted almost everywhere he preached. The Bible tells that his hearers "opposed him, abused him, and blasphemed." In another place, they were "full of wrath." He was stoned and left for dead, beaten with "many stripes," and "thrown out of the region." He was called a "pestilent fellow," a "mover of sedition," and a "ringleader" of a "sect." He was smacked in the mouth. There was "great dissension" in the crowds to which he spoke. And he was nearly "pulled in pieces" after preaching. The Bible tells us, "*All* who live Godly in Christ Jesus *shall* suffer persecution." If we are not suffering persecution, then we may not be living godly in Christ Jesus. Or we may not even be preaching the same message that Paul preached.

There goes another minute.
Gone forever. Go share your faith
while you still have time.

Never Seen Himself

Think of an eagle chick. He's climbed out of the nest. His mom wants him to fly. She wants him to step off a thousand-foot cliff. It makes sense that he's not too excited about this. He's never seen himself in a mirror. He doesn't know that God has given him wings. He has unseen muscles and perfectly positioned feathers. God has given him the ability to fly. All he has to do it take a step of faith off the high cliff to experience the purpose for which God has created him. God has given us everything we need to carry out His will. He has made us as eagles. So, don't be a chicken. Take courage. As we take that first step off that cliff to reach out to the lost, … we will find that we "mount up with wings as eagles."

There goes another minute. *Gone forever*. Go share your faith while you still have time.

Obtaining Decisions

Did you know that that your methodology reveals your theology? In other words, the method you use to share your faith reveals what you believe about God. Do you know that "salvation is of the Lord" and that "no man can come to the Son unless the Father draws him?" Then you will know that it is God who saves sinners, and we simply work with Him to reach them. We plant the seed, and He makes it grow. This frees us from determining success by how many 'decisions' we are able to get. Never forget that true evangelistic "success" is faithfully preaching the truth, the whole truth, and nothing but the truth ... in love. It is faithfully planting the seed of the Word of God in the soil of the hearts of the lost. We sow; someone waters ... but it is *God* who gives the increase.

There goes another minute.
Gone forever. **Go share your faith
while you still have time.**

Tender Conscience

It's not easy to be pure in contemporary society. Covers of magazines in bookstores and supermarkets are designed to stir up lust. All around us people use filthy words and blasphemy in everyday speech. Movies, billboards, magazines, revealing clothes bombard our eyes with things that God considers abominable. There certainly is, as the Bible says, "corruption in the world through lust."[32] So, what should we do—live in a high walled monastery? Of course not. We instead are to let our lights shine in this dark and sinful world. And we can do that by walking in the fear of the Lord, with tender consciences toward God, and by being true and faithful witnesses of Jesus Christ. So, keep close to the Lord, and make sure you reach out to this sin-loving, blind, and Hell-bent world today.

There goes another minute.
Gone forever. Go share your faith
while you still have time.

TICK ... TICK ...

Dropped by Plane

In certain states, men and women drop into forest fires and remove the fuel for which flames are looking. Without fuel, the fire will die, so these "smoke jumpers" are dropped by plane into a stricken area to cut away or burn away brush. Just over 2000 years ago, God came down from Heaven to stop a raging fire. It was the fire of wrath. The fuel that feeds the consuming fire of His holy indignation is sin. Thank God for Calvary. When Jesus cried, "It is finished," that raging fire of eternal wrath was put out for all those who repent and trust in His blood. Our salvation was at great cost, but those who neglect so great a salvation will not escape. They will pay for it with their very souls. We must warn them to make peace with God today.

There goes another minute. *Gone forever.* Go share your faith while you still have time.

TICK ...
TICK ...
TICK ...
TICK ...
TICK ...
TICK ...
TICK ...
TICK ...
TICK ...
TICK ...
TICK ...
TICK ...
TICK ...
TICK ...
TICK ...
TICK ...
TICK ...
TICK ...
TICK ...

Titanic Survivor

If you are a Christian, see yourself as a survivor of the Titanic. All around you, people are sinking into the freezing waters of death. There's room in the lifeboat. *What are you going to do?* You must make every effort to save them. *Nothing* is more important. Bible commentator, Matthew Henry, said, "The salvation of one soul is of infinitely greater importance than preserving the lives of multitudes, or promoting the welfare of a whole people. Let us in our several stations keep these things in mind, sparing no pains in God's service, and the event will prove that our labor is not in vain in the Lord. For six thousand years, He has been multiplying pardons, and yet His free grace is not tired nor grown weary. Certainly Divine mercy is an ocean that is ever full and ever flowing."

**There goes another minute.
Gone forever. Go share your faith
while you still have time.**

TICK ...
TICK ...
TICK ...
TICK ...

TICK ...
TICK ...

Peasant Pilgrimage

In Tibet, peasants make a regular pilgrimage around a sacred mountain, stopping every few steps and prostrating themselves on the rocky ground. Then they stand up and repeat the painful ritual. One woman, who had done the 32-mile pilgrimage 29 times, was asked why she did it. She said, "We want to be reborn in Heaven." How tragic that humanity thinks that by self-suffering, they can enter Heaven. They crawl on their bloodied hands and knees, fast certain foods, cut themselves, lie on beds of nails, sit on hard pews, or give money sacrificially to some worthy cause. They think that God will consider their suffering or sacrifice to be a worthy atonement for their sin. Yet, the suffering has been done. Jesus cried, "It is finished!" Because of Calvary, salvation is a free gift. How will they hear, without a preacher?

There goes another minute.
Gone forever. Go share your faith
while you still have time.

TICK ...
TICK ...
TICK ...
TICK ...
TICK ...
TICK ...
TICK ...
TICK ...
TICK ...
TICK ...
TICK ...
TICK ...
TICK ...
TICK ...
TICK ...
TICK ...
TICK ...
TICK ...
TICK ...
TICK ...
TICK ...
TICK ...
TICK ...
TICK ...
TICK ...
TICK ...
TICK ...

107

The Passion of Fear

The Scriptures warn this world, "But after your hardness and impenitent heart you treasure up to yourself wrath against the day of wrath and revelation of the righteous judgment of God; Who will render to every man according to his deeds ... to them that are contentious, and do not obey the truth, but obey unrighteousness, indignation and wrath, tribulation and anguish ..."[33] Are you warning this world that that will be a fearful thing? Isaac Watts said, "I never knew but one person in the whole course of my ministry who acknowledged that the first motions of religion in his own heart arose from a sense of the goodness of God ... But I think all besides who have come within my notice have rather been first awakened to fly from the wrath to come by the passion of fear."

There goes another minute.
Gone forever. Go share your faith
while you still have time.

Sin is Like Smog

Sin is like smog—it is not visible while you are in its midst. The Law takes the sinner above the smog of his own perspective and shows him Heaven's viewpoint. It gives him knowledge of his sin. John Bunyan warned, "The man who does not know the nature of the Law cannot know the nature of sin." Martyn Lloyd-Jones said, "The trouble with people who are not seeking for a Savior, and for salvation, is that they do not understand the nature of sin. It is the peculiar function of the Law to bring such an understanding to a man's mind and conscience. That is why great evangelical preachers 300 years ago in the time of the Puritans, and 200 years ago in the time of Whitefield and others, always engaged in what they called a preliminary 'Law work.'"

There goes another minute.
Gone forever. Go share your faith
while you still have time.

Never Despise the Law

Hopefully, you understand why God gave us The Ten Commandments. They prepare us for the One who can save us from sin and death. The Law of God prepares the soil of the human heart so that it can receive the seed of the Gospel. It convinces us of the disease, so that we can appreciate the cure. J. C. Ryle said, "Never, never let us despise [the Law]. It is the symptom of an ignorant ministry, and unhealthy state of religion, when the Law is reckoned unimportant. The true Christian delights in God's Law." In speaking of the Christian's attitude to the Law, John Wesley said, "Yea, love and value it for the sake of Him from whom it came, and of Him to whom it leads. Let it be thy glory and joy, next to the cross of Christ. Declare its praise, and make it honorable before all men."

There goes another minute.
Gone forever. Go share your faith
while you still have time.

TICK ...
TICK ...
TICK ...
TICK ...
TICK ...
TICK ...
TICK ...
TICK ...
TICK ...
TICK ...
TICK ...
TICK ...
TICK ...
TICK ...
TICK ...
TICK ...
TICK ...
TICK ...
TICK ...
TICK ...
TICK ...
TICK ...
TICK ...
TICK ...
TICK ...
TICK ...
TICK ...

Sin Becomes Trivial

If we remove the Ten Commandments out of the Gospel presentation, out goes much of sound doctrine with it. Take for example the great biblical truths that God will judge the heathen, or that Jesus is the only way to God. When the Law is removed, sin loses its true nature. It becomes trivial. This is because it is seen from man's viewpoint, rather than God's. It is the Moral Law that shows us Heaven's perspective. Without that perspective, sin loses its serious nature. Consequently, forgiveness becomes attainable through man's efforts. Heaven, without a revelation of God's perfect righteousness, comes within his grasp. But when the Law is used to show us God's perfect standard, the only way we could even hope to find peace with Him is if God Himself provided the way. And we know He did that through the cross of Jesus Christ.

There goes another minute.
Gone forever. **Go share your faith while you still have time.**

TICK ...
TICK ...
TICK ...
TICK ...
TICK ...

111

God Will Judge the Heathen

Recently, a respected preacher said that a man on an island, who had never heard of Jesus, will make it to Heaven because he had never been given a chance to reject the Savior. What about ten people on an island who have never heard the Gospel? Will they be saved without Jesus? Of course not. God will judge the heathen. He must, by nature. He will punish murderers, rapists, thieves, adulterers, and liars. Granted, being alone cuts the odds of violation of many of the Commandments, but we are sinners by nature. Lust, hatred, anger, greed, rebellion, sexual fantasies, and blasphemy don't need the presence of fellow creatures. The Bible tells us that all sin is primarily against God. So, being on an island doesn't mean that we will be free from God's wrath. Peace with God can only be found in Jesus Christ.

There goes another minute. *Gone forever.* Go share your faith while you still have time.

TICK ...
TICK ...
TICK ...
TICK ...
TICK ...
TICK ...
TICK ...
TICK ...
TICK ...
TICK ...
TICK ...
TICK ...
TICK ...
TICK ...
TICK ...
TICK ...
TICK ...

Unforgettable Cries

What do you and I *think* about? What is it that we meditate on most? It is "desire" that determines most of our thought patterns. It *should* be that the human *predicament* narrows down what we think about. Imagine a Titanic survivor. He is sitting with a few other survivors in a large, mostly empty lifeboat as the great ocean liner heaves and sinks silently beneath the freezing waters of the ocean. The only sounds that break that eerie silence are the unforgettable cries of perishing human beings pleading to be saved from an icy grave. There's plenty of room in the lifeboat. What is it then that should consume the survivor's thoughts? He should be utterly focused on saving those that are around him. *Nothing else should matter, compared to the task that is before him.*

There goes another minute.
Gone forever. Go share your faith
while you still have time.

TICK ...
TICK ...
TICK ...
TICK ...
TICK ...
TICK ...
TICK ...
TICK ...
TICK ...
TICK ...
TICK ...
TICK ...
TICK ...
TICK ...
TICK ...
TICK ...
TICK ...
TICK ...
TICK ...
TICK ...
TICK ...
TICK ...
TICK ...
TICK ...
TICK ...
TICK ...
TICK ...
TICK ...
TICK ...

You Will Leave Everything

The most important day of your life will be the day of your death. Think about that. On that day, nothing else will matter except what you have done for God and where you are going. Your house, your car, your money, your sports will mean nothing on that day. You will be leaving time and entering into eternity. Meditate on that breath-taking moment. In the exhale of one breath, you will leave everything you love. Your wedding ring. Your spouse. Your loved ones. Your vehicle. Your money. Everything. Tonight, God could say to you, "This night your soul is required of you." Let such sobering thoughts consume you. Let them drive you to use your life for what matters, to reach out to the unsaved and make a big dent in this sinful world.

There goes another minute.
Gone forever. Go share your faith
while you still have time.

Birds of a Feather

Most people keep to themselves. They are birds of a feather and they prefer to keep it that way. But not the Christian. We know that we *must* speak to strangers. Fortunately, we have the example of the way of the Master. If you study John chapter four, you will see that Jesus took the initiative by speaking *first* to the woman at the well. He didn't wait for her to ask why He had peace in His eyes, or for her to mention God. He had an agenda to share the Gospel with her, so He initiated the conversation. We have a clear agenda. We want the world to hear the Gospel and to be saved. They are not going to come to us, so we have to go to them. So, break free from the flock of shy birds and fly with the message of everlasting life.

**There goes another minute.
Gone forever. Go share your faith
while you still have time.**

Faith and Fear

TICK ...
TICK ...
TICK ...
TICK ...
TICK ...
TICK ...
TICK ...
TICK ...
TICK ...
TICK ...
TICK ...
TICK ...
TICK ...
TICK ...
TICK ...

We are in a battle for the lost. The enemy seeks to intimidate you by the use of the weapon of fear. It is meant to paralyze you. *Your* weapon is faith. It is more powerful than fear. Faith *overcomes* fear. Your concern is that if you bring up the things of God with a stranger, he will think that you are strange. He will think that you are a religious weirdo. Here's how faith works. Because you have faith in God's Word, you know that if the stranger dies in his sins, he will go to Hell ... forever. Love and concern for his eternal salvation will overcome your fear. Simply think of this reality — his worst-case scenario is the Lake of Fire; yours is that a stranger will think that you are strange. You *must* make the first move.

**There goes another minute.
Gone forever. Go share your faith
while you still have time.**

TICK ...
TICK ...
TICK ...
TICK ...
TICK ...
TICK ...

Do You Carry Tracts?

You are I are in a fight for the souls of the lost. We are told to fight the good fight of faith. Are you *armed* for battle? Do you always carry Gospel tracts? They are bullets in your gun. If you don't have any bullets, you won't have any courage. The enemy will shoot you to pieces. Here's how to enter combat. Walk up to the enemy. Give him a warm greeting. Say, "Good morning. How are you?" That will disarm him. Then draw! Whip out a tract and ask, "Did you get one of these?" The purpose of the "bullet" is to get him to surrender to your will. Your desire is to speak to him about God, and the tract will quickly get you there. So, get yourself a good reputation as one who is quick to the draw.

There goes another minute.
Gone forever. Go share your faith
while you still have time.

TICK ...
TICK ...
TICK ...
TICK ...
TICK ...
TICK ...
TICK ...
TICK ...
TICK ...
TICK ...
TICK ...
TICK ...
TICK ...
TICK ...
TICK ...
TICK ...
TICK ...
TICK ...
TICK ...
TICK ...
TICK ...
TICK ...
TICK ...
TICK ...
TICK ...
TICK ...
TICK ...
TICK ...
TICK ...
TICK ...

A Drowning Child

Oswald J. Smith said, "Can we travail for a drowning child, but not for a perishing soul? It is not hard to weep when we realize that our little one is sinking below the surface for the last time. Anguish is spontaneous then. Nor is it hard to agonize when we see the casket containing all that we love on earth borne out of the home. Ah, tears are natural at such a time. But oh, to realize and know that souls, precious, never dying souls, are perishing all around us, going out into the blackness of darkness and despair, eternally lost, and yet to feel no anguish, shed no tears, know no travail! How cold are our hearts!" Let's ask God to forgive us for such coldness toward this perishing world, and then show our concern by reaching out with the words of eternal life.

There goes another minute. *Gone forever*. Go share your faith while you still have time.

Faithful to Our Word

Have you ever said that you would pray for someone about a particular thing, and it slipped your mind? It's so easy to do. The person comes back later and says, "Thank you for praying," and you suddenly realize that you didn't pray. You didn't keep your word. That's why it's good habit to pray the moment you are asked to. As Christians, it's vital that we are faithful to our word. The Bible says that having faith in someone who doesn't do what they say they will is like having a broken tooth or a foot out of joint. Those ailments don't cause too much pain until you put pressure on them. Can God put pressure on us to reach out to the lost? Are we faithful to do His will? We must be ... if we want to hear those wonderful words, "Well done, you good and faithful servant."

There goes another minute.
Gone forever. Go share your faith
while you still have time.

TICK ...
TICK ...
TICK ...
TICK ...
TICK ...
TICK ...
TICK ...
TICK ...
TICK ...
TICK ...
TICK ...
TICK ...
TICK ...
TICK ...
TICK ...
TICK ...
TICK ...
TICK ...
TICK ...
TICK ...
TICK ...
TICK ...
TICK ...
TICK ...
TICK ...
TICK ...

119

You Can Tell a Liar

You can usually tell an unfaithful person (a liar) by what comes out of their mouth. They will often say, "I promise to have it to you by such and such a time." The key word is "promise." Liars usually have to promise because they know that their simple word isn't enough. Both Jesus and James address this. The Christian should never have to promise to do anything. If he simply says that he will do it, he will do it. His word is his bond. Psalm 15 should be inscribed on the walls of character for every man and woman of God. We can't afford not to keep our word. If we let an unsaved person down by not doing what we said, it kills our testimony. We must be blameless before a godless world if we want to have any credibility in what we preach.

**There goes another minute.
Gone forever. Go share your faith
while you still have time.**

It Took 37 Years

A Christian brother named LeeRoy Beatty memorized the entire Bible. It took him 37 years. He went to be with the Lord in 1998 at the age of 83. He used to say, "Jesus said, 'Follow me and I will make you fishers of men.' If you are not fishing, you are not following." He also said, "The Bible says, 'He that wins souls is wise.' What does that mean if you are not winning souls?" He would say, "Silence is not golden. It's yellow." He had many other pithy sayings. One was, "Don't miss Heaven. You never will forgive yourself if you do." Pithy though they were, his little sayings were based on sound doctrine. He knew his Bible. So, go fishing today. Be wise. Don't be yellow. Take courage through faith in God. Live to hear, "Well done, you good and faithful servant" and when you die, you will.

There goes another minute.
Gone forever. Go share your faith
while you still have time.

TICK ...
TICK ...
TICK ...
TICK ...
TICK ...
TICK ...
TICK ...
TICK ...
TICK ...
TICK ...
TICK ...
TICK ...
TICK ...
TICK ...
TICK ...
TICK ...
TICK ...
TICK ...
TICK ...
TICK ...
TICK ...
TICK ...
TICK ...
TICK ...
TICK ...
TICK ...
TICK ...
TICK ...

America's only Hope

We live in troubled times. America's only hope is in God. Our enemies hate us with an unprecedented intensity. Yet, Scripture makes it clear that God will not come to the rescue of a nation that gives Him lip service. America is a nation that has no fear of God. The ungodly don't fear Him because the Church has made "void" the Law. It preaches an insipid message that has no bite. It has removed the teeth of the message because they are deemed too cutting for sinners. This has resulted in few showing any interest in reaching to the lost. The message is "get what's yours in Christ." It's a self-indulgent Church that thinks only about what it can get from God. But as we read of the exploits of the early Church, we see one thing only — the Gospel of Salvation being preached to a Hell-bent world.

There goes another minute.
Gone forever. Go share your faith
while you still have time.

Strange Thoughts

Here are some strange thoughts. Where is here? Isn't it everywhere where *you* are? And that's the same for everyone. Everything and everyone else is "there." Each of us thinks that we are the center of the universe. Define "now." *When* is it? You can't. The split second that you try to pinpoint "now," it becomes "then." These thoughts are a little strange, but there *are* some things that we *can* be sure of—the sun rises; the sky is still blue; and "up" is still "up." Not true. The sun never rises. The earth turns. The sky *isn't* blue. It has no color. Neither is "up" up. Remember that the earth is round. What is up to someone at the North Pole is not up to someone at the South Pole. So many things that we think are absolutes are not. The only thing we can really trust is God's Word. Do that today.

There goes another minute.
Gone forever. Go share your faith
while you still have time.

TICK ...
TICK ...
TICK ...
TICK ...
TICK ...
TICK ...
TICK ...
TICK ...
TICK ...
TICK ...
TICK ...
TICK ...
TICK ...
TICK ...
TICK ...
TICK ...
TICK ...
TICK ...
TICK ...
TICK ...
TICK ...
TICK ...
TICK ...
TICK ...
TICK ...

The Litmus Test

Never assume that all those, who say they are Christians, are born of the Spirit. There are many tares among the wheat, foolish virgins among the wise, and bad fish among the good. They need to be awakened before the Day of Judgment, and one of the best ways to do that is to take them through "The Good Test." Ask the person if he thinks that he is a good person. It's a powerful litmus test. If he thinks he is, do what Jesus did. Take him through the Ten Commandments, and don't be afraid to let him know that if he has lied or stolen or looked with lust, he's heading for Hell. Any fear that arises in his heart because you mention his standing before God will be nothing compared to the fear he will have when he *does* stand before Him in Judgment.

There goes another minute. *Gone forever*. Go share your faith while you still have time.

Enlisted as a Firefighter

Have you ever gone out of you way to share your faith with strangers? Study what to do, and then go and do it. Then, when you return, make a point of getting on your knees and determining with all your heart to make what you have just done "a way of life." It shouldn't be a once-in-a-lifetime experience. When you became a Christian, you enlisted as a firefighter and you should have been studying how to rescue those who are about to die, and then doing it. Make sure your never fall back into complacency. You are going to "live for Christ" and work towards living for Him with even more determination than you would put into making a marriage work. You don't want to lose your first love, and if you don't continually stoke the fire, it will go out. It's just a matter of time.

There goes another minute.
Gone forever. Go share your faith
while you still have time.

TICK ...
TICK ...
TICK ...
TICK ...
TICK ...
TICK ...
TICK ...
TICK ...
TICK ...
TICK ...
TICK ...
TICK ...
TICK ...
TICK ...
TICK ...
TICK ...
TICK ...
TICK ...
TICK ...
TICK ...
TICK ...
TICK ...
TICK ...
TICK ...
TICK ...
TICK ...
TICK ...
TICK ...

125

Be Exceedingly Glad

Determine to make it a lifestyle to regularly share your faith. It may be with an unsaved friend, a coworker, a family member, or a stranger. Remember, the key to motivation is not to be concerned about yourself, but to care about the unsaved person's eternal fate. Even if you were beaten up, Jesus said to rejoice and be exceedingly glad because even the prophets before you were persecuted. Think of what a child does when he's learning to walk. If he falls down, do you discourage him from trying again? No. You want him to grow up, so you encourage him to stand on his own feet, and to take more steps. Even if he gets a bruise, you don't tell him to give up. That would be unthinkable. So, if you fall down and get bruised, stand up, dust yourself off, and take another step of faith.

**There goes another minute.
Gone forever. Go share your faith
while you still have time.**

Get Your Feet Wet

To get your feet wet in witnessing, an easy first step is learning to be friendly and talking with people. This may seem obvious, but make a habit of talking to your family members and friends regularly. Then practice being friendly with people at the park, at the gas station, or at the grocery store. If you tend to be a shy, introverted person, try to regularly open up a little and start talking with people. A simple "Hi, how are you?" isn't difficult. Or say, "Nice day, isn't it? My name is so and so … " With a bit of practice, anyone can learn to be friendly. Most people respond warmly to warmth. Then kick it up a notch by handing out some tracts. Then ask someone if they've had a Christian background. You can do it. God will help you.

There goes another minute.
Gone forever. Go share your faith
while you still have time.

TICK ...
TICK ...
TICK ...
TICK ...
TICK ...
TICK ...
TICK ...
TICK ...
TICK ...
TICK ...
TICK ...
TICK ...
TICK ...
TICK ...
TICK ...
TICK ...
TICK ...
TICK ...
TICK ...
TICK ...
TICK ...
TICK ...
TICK ...
TICK ...
TICK ...
TICK ...
TICK ...
TICK ...
TICK ...
TICK ...

Start in the Natural

To share our faith effectively, we must let people know that we are not "weirdoes" or religious fanatics. We must show them that we care, and we start by being friendly. A shy person once began greeting people by going to a park on a Saturday afternoon just to practice being friendly to strangers. He and a friend had so much fun that they couldn't wait to get out the following weekend to take the next step and actually witness to people. Try doing that, and when you have gained a measure of confidence, you can swing to the subject of spiritual things. It's not wise to walk up to people and immediately talk about Jesus. They'll most likely think you're strange. Instead, start with everyday things and then swing to the spiritual realm. That's what Jesus did in John chapter 4.

There goes another minute. *Gone forever.* Go share your faith while you still have time.

Thinking About Time

Do you ever think about "time?" What is the *dimension* of time? We measure it using clocks and watches, but we don't really give much thought as to what it is. It passes every day like the tick-tick-tick of a clock, yet we rarely consider it—until we look into the mirror and see aging lines, or we view a family photo album and think about how time flies. What is time? The dictionary doesn't help much with its definition. It just says time is "a nonspatial continuum in which events occur in apparently irreversible succession from the past through the present to the future." That's a fancy way of saying that time is something that goes on without gaps, and we have no control over it. So whatever time is, make sure you use it wisely by seeking and saving the lost.

There goes another minute.
Gone forever. Go share your faith
while you still have time.

TICK ...
TICK ...
TICK ...
TICK ...
TICK ...
TICK ...
TICK ...
TICK ...
TICK ...
TICK ...
TICK ...
TICK ...
TICK ...
TICK ...
TICK ...
TICK ...
TICK ...
TICK ...
TICK ...
TICK ...
TICK ...
TICK ...
TICK ...
TICK ...
TICK ...
TICK ...

Thinking About Eternity

Have you ever taken the time to think about the word, "eternity?" The dictionary gives it two definitions. First, it says that eternity is "time without beginning or end." Then, it says that it's "the timeless state following death." So, there you have it according to the experts. Eternity is eternal time *and* a timeless eternity. Whatever the case, we don't have time this side of eternity to haggle about what it is, because the Bible makes it clear that time is running out of time. Every tick of the clock takes us closer to the time when time will no longer exist. It will take a permanent "time out." That's why, as Christians, we should make the best use of it while we have it, and the best way we can do that is to seek and save the lost.

There goes another minute.
Gone forever. **Go share your faith while you still have time.**

It Was in a Garden

We have often spoken about having a Garden of Gethsemane experience (surrendering your will to the Lord), and how it was in another garden (the Garden of Eden) that man said, "Not Your will, but mine be done."[34] Just as there was a subtle serpent in that garden, so there is a subtle serpent ever present in your Garden of Gethsemane. The father of lies has a weapon that will make you continually sweat drops of blood: It is the weapon of fear. So, don't listen to his whispers. Every time you go to open your mouth for the Kingdom of God, you can be sure He will be there to say, "You can't do this." But when fear knocks on the door, send the Word of God to open it. Say, "I can do all things through Christ who strengthens me.[35] The Lord is my helper; I will not fear."[36]

There goes another minute.
Gone forever. **Go share your faith while you still have time.**

TICK ...
TICK ...
TICK ...
TICK ...
TICK ...
TICK ...
TICK ...
TICK ...
TICK ...
TICK ...
TICK ...
TICK ...
TICK ...
TICK ...
TICK ...
TICK ...
TICK ...
TICK ...
TICK ...
TICK ...
TICK ...
TICK ...
TICK ...
TICK ...
TICK ...
TICK ...
TICK ...
TICK ...

131

Contend For the Faith

The Bible says to "contend for the faith."[37] You will be amazed at what you can say to someone if your tone is in the spirit of gentleness. Study the New Testament to see how confrontational Jesus was when He spoke to people about their salvation. He wasn't afraid to call sin "sin," and Hell "Hell." Imitate Him. Never hesitate to use fear as a motivator for a sinner to flee to the Savior. The world will frown on this, and many within the Church may even discourage it. But any fear a person may have now because of your words of warning will be nothing compared to the fear he will have if he falls into the hands of the living God. The Lake of Fire should motivate us to cast aside our fears of rejection that come in the guise of not wanting to offend people.

There goes another minute.
Gone forever. Go share your faith
while you still have time.

The Frowns of the World

A man once took the Apostle Paul's belt, bound his own hands and feet, and said, "So shall the Jews at Jerusalem bind the man who owns this belt."[38] It was appropriate that he used a belt because he was to be persecuted for preaching uncompromising truth. The Bible speaks of the belt of truth, and Paul refused to compromise the fact that a man is justified only by faith in Jesus Christ. When we are girded about with truth, the world will hate us. If we would just say that Jesus isn't the only way to God, or that you can live a life of sin and still love God, then we would have the world's approval. Matthew Henry said, "The frowns of the world would not disquiet us, if we did not foolishly flatter ourselves with the hopes of its smiles, and court and covet them."

There goes another minute.
Gone forever. Go share your faith
while you still have time.

TICK ...
TICK ...
TICK ...
TICK ...
TICK ...
TICK ...
TICK ...
TICK ...
TICK ...
TICK ...
TICK ...
TICK ...
TICK ...
TICK ...
TICK ...
TICK ...
TICK ...
TICK ...
TICK ...
TICK ...
TICK ...
TICK ...
TICK ...
TICK ...
TICK ...
TICK ...

133

Go to the Darkness

The disciples said, "We cannot but speak the things which we have seen and heard." Think of the fate of those the enemy has "taken captive ... to do his will." While many are content with "youth night," take a team and go to the unsaved. Go to the darkness of this world with the light of the Gospel. You can even put literature in a bar and be out the door in about two minutes ... in one door, out the other before they know what's going on. Sure, your heart may tremble with fear, but if a hero isn't fearful, he's not a hero. Courage is triumphing over fear, not being free from it. Half of you will hate being there in the smoke, and the other half will weep with compassion. Ignore the "What if I get caught?" thoughts, and don't take along any weak soldiers. They can stay at home and pray.

**There goes another minute.
Gone forever. Go share your faith
while you still have time.**

You Are Greater Than John

Jesus said that John the Baptist was the greatest man to ever live.[39] He was greater than Solomon, David, Moses, and Abraham. Imagine that being said of you. When John was about the be born, it was said that he would turn "the disobedient to the wisdom of the just" and that he would "make ready a people prepared for the Lord."[40] Imagine God giving you the same incredible commission. But if you are a Christian, Jesus said that you are *greater* than John. This is because God has made you righteous in His sight through the blood of Jesus. Now your job is the same as John's. You are to turn the "disobedient to the wisdom of the just," and to "make ready a people prepared for the Lord." All you have to do to see this happen is to faithfully preach the Gospel of salvation.

There goes another minute.
Gone forever. **Go share your faith while you still have time.**

Risk-takers

The greatest achievers in life have been risk-takers. They haven't been afraid to fail. Many of life's conveniences are here because of these people. Think of the inventor of the light bulb. Edison was a risk-taker who failed many times. Peter was in this category. He stepped out of a boat and walked on water. He took a risk and broke through into the supernatural realm. That's what happens every time you step out to share your faith with an unsaved person. You take a risk. You break out of your comfort zone. But what you are doing is more important than inventing the light bulb. That invention is trapped in the temporal realm. You become involved in the *eternal* realm. Edison's light cannot enter there. Your light can. So let your little light shine today; let it shine; let it shine; let it shine.

There goes another minute. *Gone forever*. Go share your faith while you still have time.

God Be With You

Did you know that the word, "Good bye," comes from the old English words "God be with ye?" When you say those words, you are wishing that God would be with the person you are leaving. This is because if God is with them, nothing can be against them. But, if God is against you, nothing can be for you. And if you are not a Christian, He is against you, because you have transgressed His Law a multitude of times. You are like a criminal who has committed heinous crimes. Death will arrest you; the Law will condemn you; and the judge will sentence you. But if you *are* a Christian, God has dismissed your case. Now you are commissioned to tell the world that the Judge can commute their death sentence, and you have the promise that God will be with you.

There goes another minute.
Gone forever. Go share your faith
while you still have time.

TICK ...
TICK ...
TICK ...
TICK ...
TICK ...

137

TICK ...
TICK ...

Never a Man Spoke Like This Man

TICK ...
TICK ...
TICK ...
TICK ...
TICK ...
TICK ...
TICK ...
TICK ...
TICK ...
TICK ...
TICK ...
TICK ...
TICK ...
TICK ...
TICK ...
TICK ...

Once the Pharisees sent out officers to arrest Jesus, but they returned empty-handed, saying, "Never a man spoke like this man."[41] Look at His words: "I am the way, the truth and the life. I am the resurrection and the life. I am come that they might have life. He than believes on me has everlasting life. He that has seen me has seen the Father. I came down from Heaven. I am the light of the world." Never a man spoke like this Man, because this was no ordinary man. This was God in human form, and He came to this earth to destroy the power of death. If we know this, if we have experienced His power in our lives, if we have been saved from death, then how can we not say with the disciples, "We cannot but speak that which we have seen and heard!"?

TICK ...
TICK ...
TICK ...
TICK ...

**There goes another minute.
Gone forever. Go share your faith
while you still have time.**

TICK ...
TICK ...
TICK ...
TICK ...
TICK ...
TICK ...
TICK ...
TICK ...

None That Seek After God

Do you know that the First Commandment demands that we love God with all of our hearts, minds, souls, and strength? When we tell the world what that Commandment requires, it shows them that they have fallen short of God's standard. The Moral Law reveals that they don't love God, even though He gave them life. The Bible says that there is none that seek after God, that they are unthankful and unholy, and are "children of disobedience." The Law of God brings the knowledge of sin. It calls for our blood, and demands our death and damnation. When a sinful world understands that, they are ready for the Good News that Christ redeemed us from the curse of the Law, being made a curse for us.[42] The Law makes the cross make sense. That's why Jesus used it. That's why Paul used it. Do the same.

There goes another minute.
Gone forever. **Go share your faith while you still have time.**

TICK ...
TICK ...
TICK ...
TICK ...
TICK ...
TICK ...
TICK ...
TICK ...
TICK ...
TICK ...
TICK ...
TICK ...
TICK ...
TICK ...
TICK ...
TICK ...
TICK ...
TICK ...
TICK ...
TICK ...
TICK ...
TICK ...
TICK ...
TICK ...
TICK ...
TICK ...
TICK ...
TICK ...
TICK ...
TICK ...

Laying Down Our Weapons

If you are in the habit of challenging sinners to "ask Jesus into your life," you might like to rethink what you are saying. You might instead like to tell them that they need to *surrender* to Jesus as Lord and Savior. When someone asks Jesus into "their life," it is still "their" life. But when he or she *surrenders* to Him, they "give up" their life. The essence of conversion is to surrender to God. It is to lay down our weapons of hostility, and to lift up our hands in surrender. It is to give up your life. Paul said, "I am crucified with Christ: nevertheless I live; yet not I, but Christ lives in me: and the life which I now live in the flesh I live by the faith of the Son of God, who loved me, and gave himself for me."[43]

There goes another minute.
Gone forever. **Go share your faith while you still have time.**

John's Vision

Much of the modern Church has failed to warn their hearers to flee from the wrath to come. John Wesley said, "I desire to have both Heaven and Hell in my eye." In other words, he wasn't happy merely to get his ticket to Heaven without reaching out to those who were under the fire of the wrath of God. He caught a glimpse of the wrath of God on sinners. The Bible says that in John's vision of the Day of wrath, "... mighty men, and every slave, and every free man hid themselves in the dens and in the rocks of the mountains, and said to the mountains and rocks, fall on us and hide us from the face of Him that sits on the throne and from the wrath of the Lamb; for the great day of His wrath is come, and who shall be able to stand?"[44]

There goes another minute.
Gone forever. Go share your faith
while you still have time.

Anger Without Cause

The Sixth of the Ten Commandments says, "You shall not kill." Do you ever use the Commandments with the lost? Paul used three in Romans chapter two, and he told us to imitate him. Jesus said that if we get anger without cause, we are in danger of Judgment. The Bible further says that if we hate our brother, we have committed murder. When we tell the world what the Commandments require, it shows them that they have fallen short of God's standard. The Law of God brings the knowledge of sin. It calls for our blood, and demands our death and damnation. When a sinful world understands that, they are ready for the Good News of the cross. It is the Law makes the cross make sense. That's why Jesus used it. That's why Paul used it. Do the same.

**There goes another minute.
Gone forever. Go share your faith
while you still have time.**

Touching Jesus

The Bible tells us, " ... a woman who had a flow of blood for twelve years came from behind and touched the hem of [the] garment [of Jesus]; for she said to herself, 'If only I may touch His garment, I shall be made well.'"[45] It was the knowledge that she wasn't well that made her press in to touch the Savior. The reason sinners don't see their need for the grace of God in Christ is that they don't see that they are not well. They are diseased, and deceived by the disease of and the deceitfulness of sin. John MacArthur said, "God's grace cannot be faithfully preached to unbelievers until the Law is preached, and man's corrupt nature is exposed. It is impossible for a person to fully realize his need for God's grace until he sees how terribly he has failed the standards of God's Law."

There goes another minute.
Gone forever. **Go share your faith while you still have time.**

The Name of the Lord

The Third of the Ten Commandments forbids taking the Name of the Lord in vain, and warns that the Lord will not hold him guiltless who takes His name in vain. Jesus even said that a man will have to give an account of every idle word spoken.[46] When we tell sinners what the Commandments require, it shows them that they have fallen short of God's standard. The Law of God brings the knowledge of sin. It reveals that God sees every deed and hears every word, and will bring them all into judgment. The Law calls for our blood, and demands our death sentence. When a rebellious world understands that, they are ready to hear that Christ redeemed us from the curse of the Law, being made a curse for us. The Law makes the cross make sense. That's why Jesus used it. That's why Paul used it. Do the same.

There goes another minute.
Gone forever. **Go share your faith**
while you still have time.

Big Black Clouds

There's something wonderful about the atmosphere moments after a thunderstorm. Big black clouds begin to roll back, and bright beams of sunlight burst through the clean air. There's a freshness in the heavens. A rainbow arches across the sky as birds begin to sing. That's how grace and Law work together. There's something incredibly wonderful about what happens in the heart of sinner after he has stood beneath the thundering of God's Law. Moments earlier, flashes of His wrath terrified his heart, after he understood his guilt before a holy God. Grace moves the black clouds of wrath away, and suddenly beams of the light of Calvary's love burst through the atmosphere. The beautiful rainbow of God's exceedingly great and precious promises arch across eternity. There is a song of forgiveness. There's freshness in the air. Old things pass away, behold, all things are become new.

There goes another minute.
Gone forever. **Go share your faith while you still have time.**

TICK ...
TICK ...
TICK ...
TICK ...
TICK ...
TICK ...
TICK ...
TICK ...
TICK ...
TICK ...
TICK ...
TICK ...
TICK ...
TICK ...
TICK ...
TICK ...
TICK ...
TICK ...
TICK ...
TICK ...
TICK ...
TICK ...
TICK ...
TICK ...
TICK ...
TICK ...
TICK ...
TICK ...

145

Sin is Like Quicksand

Sin is like quicksand. It's the devil's playground. It lies before the unsuspecting sinner as an unseen deathtrap. As he steps into it, he begins to sink, and with each movement of his flesh, it takes him deeper into its subtle embrace. In a moment, he's gone. Sucked beneath the silence of the grave. Gone forever into the horror of Hell. The only way to get out of quicksand is to have someone, who is not in its power, to pull us out. Thank God that the hand of grace is willing to save us from the terrors of Hell. This is what the Apostle Paul speaks of in Romans chapters 7 and 8. His struggle against the power of sin only took him deeper into its cold embrace. He cried, "Who will free me from this body of death!" and then sang the praise of Him who reached into death itself to pull him out of its grip.

There goes another minute.
Gone forever. **Go share your faith
while you still have time.**

Hell Will Freeze Over

It seems that the world talks about Hell far more than the Church. It speaks of the fires of Hell when it says, "Hell will freeze over..." and of its inevitability by saying, "As *sure* as Hell." They even admit to man's indebtedness to the Law of God by saying, "There will be Hell to pay," and rattle off phrases such as, "I'll be damned." Such talk is insane. They don't believe God's Word and yet they adopt its language. How can they be so flippant about the judgment of Almighty God? The Bible tells us how. There is no fear of God before their eyes. They are blinded and held captive by the devil. The only hope of their rescue is the grace of God, and that's still available in Jesus Christ. He takes off the blinders, breaks the chains, and sets the captives free.

There goes another minute.
Gone forever. Go share your faith
while you still have time.

TICK ...
TICK ...
TICK ...
TICK ...
TICK ...
TICK ...
TICK ...
TICK ...
TICK ...
TICK ...
TICK ...
TICK ...
TICK ...
TICK ...
TICK ...
TICK ...
TICK ...
TICK ...
TICK ...
TICK ...
TICK ...
TICK ...
TICK ...
TICK ...
TICK ...
TICK ...
TICK ...

The Lord My God

Study closely the biblical phrase, "The Lord your God." Throughout the thousands of years of Scripture, it doesn't change. God is *the* Lord, *our* God. That is, He is the supreme authority—the Lord. But even though He is the God of all humanity, their Creator, He's not their *Lord* until they yield to His Lordship. But the phrase suddenly changes when Thomas sees the risen Savior. He cries *"My* Lord and *my* God." The transformation comes when blind, willful unbelief yields to saving faith in Jesus. The world acknowledges that God is their Creator, but to be saved, they must yield to Him as Lord, and the way to have them do that is to introduce their blind and unbelieving hearts to the risen Savior. That's our great commission—to preach Christ the Lord, the risen Savior, the conqueror of death and of Hell.

**There goes another minute.
Gone forever. Go share your faith
while you still have time.**

Stay At Home

When Gideon was told by God to form an army, He cut it down in size. The fearful were told to go home. Those who didn't look out for the enemy while drinking water were dismissed. The rest were instructed to break vessels in the darkness, so that their lights would shine. Then they were to lift up their voices in a shout. Have you enlisted into the Army of God, and yet are more concerned about your fears than you are about the fate of the lost? Then stay at home and pray. Do you believe that you are in a spiritual battle against unseen demonic powers? If not, then you had better stay home. But if you believe in the cause of the Gospel, then be a broken vessel and let your light shine. Lift up your voice as a trumpet and show this people their transgressions.

**There goes another minute.
Gone forever. Go share your faith
while you still have time.**

TICK ...
TICK ...
TICK ...
TICK ...
TICK ...
TICK ...
TICK ...
TICK ...
TICK ...
TICK ...
TICK ...
TICK ...
TICK ...
TICK ...
TICK ...
TICK ...
TICK ...
TICK ...
TICK ...
TICK ...
TICK ...
TICK ...
TICK ...
TICK ...
TICK ...
TICK ...
TICK ...

The Good Lord

The world has a language it uses when it speaks of God. If they say grace before a meal on TV or in the movies, you can be sure they won't say, "In Jesus' name, Amen." Or when they speak about God, they will call Him, "The Man upstairs," or the old faithful, "The Good Lord." They think somehow that if God is good, He will be good enough to overlook their sins and drop any thought of having a Judgment Day. Yet, their own words condemn them. It is because of the goodness of God that there is going to be a judgment. His goodness demands that justice be done. What judge could be considered good who didn't see that justice was done? So, may you and I stand up and tell them the truth, that they have to face perfect goodness on the Day of Wrath, and for that they need a Savior.

There goes another minute.
Gone forever. **Go share your faith while you still have time.**

Do As You Please

Someone once said, "If I had my way in this world, I would have it so that all would be allowed to do as they please." That sounds ideal ... until someone is pleased to steal from me, or it pleases him to kill another human being. The problem is that sin dwells in our hearts and while it promises pleasure, it's in truth "the ultimate party-pooper." Sin is the undetected poison hidden in a delicious meal. Paul spoke of sin deceiving him and bringing about his death. John Bunyan (author of *Pilgrim's Progress*) said, "The man who does not know the nature of the Law, cannot know the nature of sin." And Martin Luther added, "The first duty of the Gospel preacher is to declare God's Law and show the nature of sin." So, take courage, and take the Law and use it to show sinners the true and deceiving nature of sin.

There goes another minute.
Gone forever. Go share your faith
while you still have time.

TICK ...
TICK ...
TICK ...
TICK ...
TICK ...
TICK ...
TICK ...
TICK ...
TICK ...
TICK ...
TICK ...
TICK ...
TICK ...
TICK ...
TICK ...
TICK ...
TICK ...
TICK ...
TICK ...
TICK ...
TICK ...
TICK ...
TICK ...
TICK ...
TICK ...
TICK ...

151

A Lot of Praying

Sometimes we think that all God requires of us is that we pray for this world. Prayer is good, but God has chosen "The foolishness of *preaching* to save them that believe."[47] We are asked, "How will they hear without a *preacher*?"[48] Are you that vessel that has said to God, "Here I am Lord, send me"?[49] Are you prepared to come out of the prayer closet and obey the Great Commission? A. W. Tozer said, "Have you noticed how much praying for revival has been going on of late—and how little revival has resulted? I believe the problem is that we have been trying to substitute praying for obeying, and it simply will not work. To pray for revival while ignoring the plain precept laid down in Scripture is to waste a lot of words and get nothing for our trouble. Prayer will become effective when we stop using it as a substitute for obedience."

**There goes another minute.
Gone forever. Go share your faith
while you still have time.**

The Cross Should Be Raised

George MacLeod was a great preacher who, hundreds of years ago, faithfully obeyed the Great Commission. He exalted Jesus Christ in his preaching and wasn't afraid to preach the blood of the cross. He said, "I simply argue that the cross should be raised at the center of the marketplace as well as on the steeple of the church. I am recovering the claim that Jesus was not crucified in a cathedral between two candles, but on a cross between two thieves; on the town's garbage heap; at a crossroad, so cosmopolitan they had to write His title in Hebrew and Latin and Greek … at the kind of a place where cynics talk smut, and thieves curse, and soldiers gamble. Because that is where He died. And that is what He died for. And that is what He died about. That is where church-men ought to be and what church-men ought to be about."

There goes another minute.
Gone forever. Go share your faith
while you still have time.

The Family Meal

In November 2004, *CBS News* reported that studies showed that children who ate regular meals with their parents were less likely to smoke cigarettes, drink alcohol, take drugs, get depressed, or commit suicide. Even the world can see that family meal times are informal gatherings when you not only communicate with those you love, but share personal time with them. As Christians, we need to take that gathering time past mere communication. By gathering around God's Word in family devotions, we are fortifying that communicative relationship even more, and taking it from the temporal realm into the eternal. But our times as family should also be used to impart concern for the unsaved. If we couldn't care less about the fate of the lost, then we will reproduce our own kind. We want to see our children loving to do God's will. We want children to whom we can say, " "

There goes another minute.
Gone forever. **Go share your faith while you still have time.**

TICK ... TICK ...

That Eerie Silence

The Bible says that as a man "thinks in his heart, so is he."[50] What do we *think* about? Think about it—what is it that we meditate on? It is "desire" that determines most of our thought patterns. It *should* be that the human predicament narrows down what we think about. Imagine a shipwreck survivor as he sits with two or three other survivors in a huge and mostly empty lifeboat. As the great ocean liner heaves, and sinks silently beneath the freezing waters of the ocean, the only sounds that break that eerie silence are the unforgettable cries of perishing human beings, pleading to be saved from an icy grave. What is it then that should consume the survivor's thoughts? What should be his greatest *desire*? He should be utterly focused on saving those that are dying around him. *Nothing else should matter, compared to the task that is before him.*

**There goes another minute.
Gone forever. Go share your faith
while you still have time.**

Apologizing for God

A major U.S. denomination produced a pamphlet in which they talked about sin. But because they didn't use the God's Law to bring the knowledge of sin, they almost apologized for God and His requirements. They said, "Not that you're necessarily a bad person, but still ... His standards are higher than you can reach. As the Bible says with some bluntness, '... All have sinned and fall short of the glory of God.'" But the *Bible* says that our hearts are more than "bad;" they are "deceitfully wicked."[51] We are enemies of God in our minds. Our carnal mind is in a state of hostility toward God and His Law. The problem is that humanity is blind to the truth about sin, until the Law gives us much-needed light. May you and I learn to take the light of the Law and use it as Jesus did.

There goes another minute. *Gone forever.* Go share your faith while you still have time.

The Aging Process

Imagine that you turned on the news tonight and heard that scientists have developed a pill that stops the aging process. The pill works. It *immediately* reverses the programming in human genes. This means that you can live to 100 years and still keep your youthful looks, your eyesight, your hearing, your hair, your energy, and your mind. Imagine if science did come up with a *genuine* anti-aging drug. What in the world would you pay for it? No one wants to grow old and die. Here's another thought-provoking question for the unsaved. If there was one chance in a million that the Bible is right when it says, "Jesus Christ has abolished death,"[52] don't you owe it to your good sense just to look into it? When we say that to the lost, we appeal to their will to live. Do that today with someone you care about.

There goes another minute. *Gone forever.* Go share your faith while you still have time.

Life-sustaining Food

Consider for a moment the words of Jesus to His disciples shortly after He spoke to the woman at the well: "But He said to them, 'I have food to eat of which you do not know'" Then He said, "My food is to do the will of Him who sent Me, and to finish His work."[53] He had just done the will of the Father by sharing the words of everlasting life with the woman at the well. Doing that was to Jesus as if He had just eaten life-sustaining food. You can know that same fulfilling joy as you obey the command, "Go into all the world and preach the Gospel to every creature."[54] As you do so, watch "the Philemon 1:6 principle" begin to take effect in your life. According to that verse, your understanding and appreciation of every good thing we have in the Lord will deepen.

**There goes another minute.
Gone forever. Go share your faith
while you still have time.**

TICK ... TICK ...

A Full Understanding

Listen to how the Amplified Bible translates Philemon 1:6: "[And I pray] that the participation in and sharing of your faith may produce and promote full recognition and appreciation and understanding and precise knowledge of every good [thing] that is ours in [our identification with] Christ Jesus [and unto His glory]." The implications are very clear. If you and I want more full understanding of every good thing we have in Christ, we can get it by sharing our faith. "Give and it shall be given to you"[55] isn't necessarily referring to financial return. The Scriptures say that when we share our faith, it actually *produces* that knowledge in us. Matthew Henry said, "I would think it a greater happiness to gain one soul to Christ than mountains of silver and gold to myself." Charles Spurgeon said, "To be a soul winner is the happiest thing in this world."

There goes another minute.
Gone forever. **Go share your faith while you still have time.**

Take a Break, Honey

Here are some interpretations of the language of a husband: "Take a break, honey; you're working too hard." That really means: "I can't hear the game over the vacuum cleaner." Here's another thing husbands tend to say: "That's interesting, dear." It really means: "Are you still talking?" One more: "Honey, you look terrific." That one really means: "Please don't try on one more outfit. I'm starving." That's marriage talk, and it carries a hidden meaning, but when we talk with the unsaved, the Bible says, "We use great plainness of speech."[56] We can't have a hidden agenda or use doubletalk. We must make known the issues of eternity with unparalleled clarity, and the best way to do that is to do what the Bible says—to study until you become a workman or women who needs not be ashamed. Study the principles used by Jesus, and then imitate Him.

There goes another minute.
Gone forever. Go share your faith
while you still have time.

Lower the Law

John Newton (the man who wrote "Amazing Grace") said, "Ignorance of the nature and design of the Law is at the bottom of most religious mistakes." Charles Spurgeon (the Prince of Preachers) added, "I do not believe that any man can preach the Gospel who does not preach the Law ... Lower the Law and you dim the light by which man perceives his guilt; this is a very serious loss to the sinner rather than a gain; for it lessens the likelihood of his conviction and conversion. I say you have deprived the Gospel of its ablest auxiliary [most powerful weapon] when you have set aside the Law. You have taken away from it the schoolmaster that is to bring men to Christ ...They will never accept grace till they tremble before a just and holy Law. Therefore the Law serves a most necessary purpose, and it must not be removed from its place."

There goes another minute.
Gone forever. Go share your faith
while you still have time.

TICK ...
TICK ...
TICK ...
TICK ...
TICK ...
TICK ...
TICK ...
TICK ...
TICK ...
TICK ...
TICK ...
TICK ...
TICK ...
TICK ...
TICK ...
TICK ...
TICK ...
TICK ...
TICK ...
TICK ...
TICK ...
TICK ...
TICK ...
TICK ...

When Things Go Wrong

Have you a relationship with God where it's second nature for you to talk to God about everything? We are told to pray without ceasing, but some are too busy to pray ... *until things go wrong.* That sort of prayer treats God like a butler, when *we* are the ones who should be the servants of God. A man was once chopping down a tree with a blunt axe. A friend suggested that he stop for a moment to sharpen his axe. He replied, *"I'm trying to chop down this tree. I haven't got time to stop and sharpen the axe!"* If he would only stop for a moment and sharpen the axe, he would slice through the tree with greater ease. Whatever you have to do each day, stop and sharpen the axe through prayer. You will slice through the day with great ease. Then devote the time you save to reaching the lost.

There goes another minute.
Gone forever. **Go share your faith
while you still have time.**

Grime on the Face

Think what would happen to a man who never looked into a mirror. It wouldn't be long until he became unaware that he had grime on his face. The same applies spiritually. Sin is like bad breath or body odor. We can detect it in others, but not so easily in ourselves. That's why we need to look into the mirror of God's Word under the light of a tender conscience and a willingness to listen to it. Check the Bible out daily to see if any cleaning needs to be done. Do we meet the standards of what Christians should be like, or is there sin staining our flesh? The person who continually studies the Scriptures is aware of his faults because he says with the psalmist, "Search me, O God, and know my heart. Try me, and know my thoughts, and see if there be any wicked way in me."[57]

There goes another minute.
Gone forever. Go share your faith
while you still have time.

The Responsible Nose

Did you know that the nose is responsible for millions of people speaking to strangers who normally wouldn't say a word to each other? If you don't believe me, try sneezing in public almost anywhere in the world, and listen to strangers say, "God bless you!" Complete strangers will ask God to bless you, simply because your nose decided to clear itself. We are living in a day when any talk about God and creation is left out of public education, yet there was a time when most school children knew the Ten Commandments. They had a moral compass. But the Moral Law does more than that. It reveals the holy standard of God. It shows us how far we have fallen short of the glory of God. It reveals sin in its true light and how desperately we need God's mercy in Christ, so use it today for that purpose.

There goes another minute.
Gone forever. **Go share your faith while you still have time.**

TICK ...
TICK ...
TICK ...
TICK ...
TICK ...
TICK ...
TICK ...
TICK ...
TICK ...
TICK ...
TICK ...
TICK ...
TICK ...
TICK ...
TICK ...
TICK ...
TICK ...
TICK ...
TICK ...
TICK ...
TICK ...
TICK ...
TICK ...
TICK ...
TICK ...

The Conscience Bears Witness

What do you say to someone who says, "There's no God?" You reason with him that every building has a builder, and that every painting has a painter. Even a child can understand that. Then you swing from his intellect to his conscience. You need to do this to be effective in reasoning with him because, according to Romans 8:7, his carnal mind is in a state of hostility toward God. The following verse says that his hostility is directed towards God's Moral Law. So, you must learn to speak to his conscience. Romans 2:15 tell us that the conscience "bears witness" with the Law. So, when you say, "You know it's wrong to lie and steal, don't you?" his conscience bears witness, and when conscience begins to do that, it's the first step toward an awareness of the true nature of sin, and the need for God's forgiveness.

There goes another minute.
Gone forever. Go share your faith
while you still have time.

TICK ...
TICK ...
TICK ...
TICK ...
TICK ...
TICK ...
TICK ...
TICK ...
TICK ...
TICK ...
TICK ...
TICK ...
TICK ...
TICK ...
TICK ...
TICK ...
TICK ...
TICK ...
TICK ...
TICK ...
TICK ...
TICK ...
TICK ...
TICK ...
TICK ...
TICK ...
TICK ...
TICK ...

165

The Hammer of Death

Listen to these words from Martin Luther: "As long as a person is not a murderer, adulterer, thief, he would swear that he is righteous. How is God going to humble such a person except by the Law? The Law is the hammer of death, the thunder of Hell and the thunder of God's wrath to bring down the proud and shameless hypocrites. When the Law was instituted on Mount Sinai it was accompanied by lightning, by storms, by the sounds of trumpets, to tear to pieces that monster called self-righteousness. As long as a person thinks he is right, he is going to be incomprehensibly proud and presumptuous. He is going to hate God, despise His grace and mercy, and ignore the promises in Christ." So, learn to do what Jesus did. Use the Ten Commandments to show sinners that they need a Savior, or they will perish.

There goes another minute. *Gone forever.* **Go share your faith while you still have time.**

Throwing Dust in the Eyes

Most don't realize that we, as a Church, have moved far away from biblical evangelism. Many of today's preachers are merely motivational speakers. They present God as a divine butler. Rarely is there reference to God's Law and the nature of sin. But listen to A. W. Pink. He said, "Without [the preaching of the Law] the preacher is building a house which will not stand; yea, he is throwing dust in the eyes of the people, bolstering them up in a false hope. Until the Law is given its proper place in the pulpit, and is preached regularly, plainly, authoritatively, the tide of lawlessness, which has swept over this favored land (and throughout all the so-called 'civilized nations'), will continue rising higher and higher. Well may we pray, 'It is time for Thee, Lord, to work: *for they have made void Thy law.*'"

There goes another minute.
Gone forever. Go share your faith
while you still have time.

The Sin of Unbelief

In the Gospel of Luke, the Bible tells us that John the Baptist's father was struck dumb because of the sin of unbelief. He insulted God by not believing His promises. Perhaps you are like Zacharius. You have been struck dumb and can't speak to the unsaved, because you don't believe that God can help you reach the lost. If that's your case, do what Zacharius did. He called for a writing tablet. He found another means of communicating what he wanted to say. So, if you can't speak, don't stay dumb. Say what you want to say by writing a letter. Send an email. You can do that. Or drop tracts in places where sinners will find them. When Zacharius communicated what he had to say, the Bible tells us that he suddenly found his voice and glorified God. May that be your experience.

**There goes another minute.
Gone forever. Go share your faith
while you still have time.**

Sharing Out of Guilt

Some people ask the question, "Is it wrong that I share my faith out of a motive of guilt? Shouldn't I simply want to please God, and seek the lost because of that motive alone?" The answer is that we *should* have a pure motive for reaching the lost, but often we don't. Think of a firefighter. The person he climbs a ladder to rescue couldn't care less about his motive for saving them from being burned to death by the terrifying flames. He may be up there because he wants to please his fire chief, or he may be there because he felt guilty snoozing in the fire station when people needed to be rescued. *Why* he's there is of little consequence. All that matters is the fact that he *is* there. So, don't get caught up in *why* you should be reaching out to the lost. Just do it.

There goes another minute. *Gone forever.* Go share your faith while you still have time.

TICK ...
TICK ...
TICK ...
TICK ...
TICK ...
TICK ...
TICK ...
TICK ...
TICK ...
TICK ...
TICK ...
TICK ...
TICK ...
TICK ...
TICK ...
TICK ...
TICK ...
TICK ...
TICK ...
TICK ...
TICK ...
TICK ...
TICK ...
TICK ...
TICK ...
TICK ...
TICK ...

Our Own Conceit

The Bible warns us, "Be not wise in your own conceits."[58] Conceit is a subtle sin that can hinder us from being effective for the Kingdom of God. The Greek word means, "to be wise in your own opinions." It whispers, "There's nothing much you don't know." Matthew Henry said, "It is good to be wise, but it is bad to think ourselves so." Someone once said, "In order to keep a true perspective of one's importance, everyone should have a dog to worship him and a cat to ignore him." A know-it-all attitude can even be damaging to our testimony if it becomes evident when we witness to an unsaved person and it sounds condescending. Instead, we should obey the Scriptures and not think of ourselves more highly than we ought to think ... and nothing keeps us low to the ground like gazing up at the cross.

There goes another minute. *Gone forever.* Go share your faith while you still have time.

An Old Soldier

There are some who say that "repentance" is an old-fashioned word that the world cannot understand. However, we must be careful to check our motives for wanting to find a more acceptable word. "Sin" is also an old-fashioned word that the world cannot understand. Do we want to change words to help the world understand them, or do we want to somehow shake off the reproach that comes with their use? If the world cannot understand the meaning of spiritual words, then we should explain what the words mean. Sin is transgression of the Law (1 John 3:4), and repentance means, "to turn from sin." It is more than contrition (sorrow for sin). It means, "to confess it and forsake it." An old soldier once summed up repentance. He said, "God said 'Attention! Halt! About turn! Quick march!'"

There goes another minute.
Gone forever. Go share your faith
while you still have time.

TICK ... (repeated down the left margin)

An Ignorant Man

An ignorant man looks at a beautiful painting and sees a painting. An insightful man will look at the same painting and see the genius of the painter's hand. When someone becomes a Christian, he no longer looks at the beauty of sunrise and merely sees a sunrise. He sees the genius of the creative hand of Almighty God. The eyes of his understanding are enlightened.[59] The entire creation is the canvas of the Creator. He is born again, like a man born blind who suddenly receives his sight. He realizes that Heaven is real, and then it strikes him that Hell is also real. From that moment, he not only sees the beauty of God's creation. He looks past it … into eternity. He now has a divine mandate: to urgently and passionately seek and save the lost.

There goes another minute.
Gone forever. **Go share your faith while you still have time.**

The Brain Stem

For years, high-speed racing car drivers have been instantly killed when violent accidents have pulled their "brain stems" loose. But when Dr. Robert Hubbard invented a head harness that stopped that from happening, seven-time NASCAR champion, Dale Earnhardt, mockingly said to a friend, "I haven't pulled my brain stem loose." As he approached the final bend in the Daytona 500 in February of 2001, he crashed and was instantly killed when his brain stem was loosened. From that time onward, the device was made mandatory in racing cars. Its inventor said, "As soon as I realized that it would work ... I became a fanatic. I quietly resolved to continue working ... until it was used commonly." We have discovered the answer to death itself. How much more should we be fanatical in quiet resolve to reach the lost?

There goes another minute.
Gone forever. Go share your faith
while you still have time.

TICK ...
TICK ...
TICK ...
TICK ...
TICK ...
TICK ...
TICK ...
TICK ...
TICK ...
TICK ...
TICK ...
TICK ...
TICK ...
TICK ...
TICK ...
TICK ...
TICK ...
TICK ...
TICK ...
TICK ...
TICK ...
TICK ...
TICK ...
TICK ...
TICK ...
TICK ...
TICK ...
TICK ...

The Holiness of God

The ignorance of human nature is optimized by those who say that they will believe in God if He will appear to them. But if God appeared to them, they would instantly die. His holiness would consume them faster than the surface of the sun would melt already soft butter. Not only that, but God doesn't require that we "believe" in Him. The Bible says that demons believe in God and tremble. Besides, all men already believe in Him. He has given light to *every* man[60]; it's just that there are some that the Scriptures call "fools" who deny their inbuilt knowledge of God's existence.[61] Salvation comes from more than a mere belief. It comes when we obey God by turning from sin and trusting in the Savior. It's then that sinners are forgiven their sins and granted the gift of everlasting life.

There goes another minute.
Gone forever. **Go share your faith while you still have time.**

Who Made God?

Who made God! That's often asked as a statement rather than a question, because the questioner doesn't think it has an answer. But it does. No one made God. He has no beginning and no end. He's like space. It has no beginning and no end. It's mind-boggling, but when we realize that God doesn't dwell in the dimension of time, it helps to make it make sense. He dwells in "eternity," where there is no time. You can see through Bible prophecy that God can flick through time as we flick through the pages of a book. He knows the beginning from the end. But because we are held in the dimension of time, logic demands that everything must have a beginning and an end. Not so in eternity, and that's the dimension we will enter when we pass through death.

There goes another minute.
Gone forever. Go share your faith
while you still have time.

The Old Testament God

Some people think that the God of the Old Testament and the God of the New Testament are different. They think that in the Old Testament, He was wrath-filled, but in the New Testament, He lightened up and become more congenial. No so. The Bible says He *never* changes. God is just as merciful and kind in the Old Testament, and just as wrath-filled in the New. If you don't believe it, see how He killed a husband and wife in the Book of Acts simply because they told one lie.[62] Read the Book of Revelation and you will see wrath on almost every page. But His fury was never seen so clearly as at the cross. It was there that His righteous anger against sin was revealed. Wrath was poured on the Savior so that we could have mercy. He suffered and died, so that we could be blessed and live.

There goes another minute. *Gone forever*. Go share your faith while you still have time.

Jesus and Anger

Jesus was without sin, but say that to a sinner and he will probably tell you that Jesus sinned when He cleared the temple. Jesus *did* become angry, but the Bible speaks of a sinful anger that has no cause.[63] Jesus had *good* cause to be angry. Money-hungry televangelists had set up shop in the temple of God, and Jesus cleared them out with a whip. Wouldn't you like to have been a fly on the wall that day? Jesus was no girly-man. He had the strong hands of a carpenter, and a stronger love for righteousness. He cleared the temple of thieves, and that's what He wants to do with sinners. The thief who came to kill, steal, and destroy must be driven from the hearts of guilty sinners, so that they can become the temple of the Holy Spirit.

There goes another minute.
Gone forever. Go share your faith
while you still have time.

TICK ...
TICK ...
TICK ...
TICK ...
TICK ...
TICK ...
TICK ...
TICK ...
TICK ...
TICK ...
TICK ...
TICK ...
TICK ...
TICK ...
TICK ...
TICK ...
TICK ...
TICK ...
TICK ...
TICK ...
TICK ...
TICK ...
TICK ...
TICK ...
TICK ...
TICK ...
TICK ...

177

Divided Light

In the beginning, God created the heavens and the earth. There was darkness, and the Spirit of God moved, and created light. Then He divided light from darkness. If you are a Christian, it's because the Spirit of God "moved." He sought us out in the darkness and brought us into the light. "For God, who commanded the light to shine out of darkness, has shined in our hearts, to give the light of the knowledge of the glory of God in the face of Jesus Christ."[64] He gave us a new beginning, and then divided the light from the darkness. Now we can walk either in the darkness or in the light. "For you were once darkness, but now you are light in the Lord. Walk as children of light."[65] And we can best do that by preaching "the light of the Gospel of the glory of Christ."

There goes another minute.
Gone forever. Go share your faith
while you still have time.

Is God Unjust?

Sometimes some people suggest that God is unfair, in that He is going to send sweet little old ladies to Hell along with evil people like Adolph Hitler. In other words, they accuse God of being unjust. Those who suggest such a thing need not be concerned. God will do the right thing on the Day of Judgment. He will give every man and woman exactly what he or she deserves He will judge the world "in righteousness."[66] Little old ladies, who have had a lifetime to amass a "multitude" of sins, will be in big trouble if they die in their sins without a Savior to wash them clean. So if you are ever asked about this issue, answer it and then do what Jesus did in Luke 13: Take the person who asked the question back to *their* responsibility before God and their need of a Savior.

There goes another minute.
Gone forever. **Go share your faith**
while you still have time.

TICK ...

A Sword to the Throat

TICK ...

TICK ...

TICK ...

What do you do if someone says that they don't believe the Bible? If that happens, don't worry. It is still quick and powerful even if someone says they don't believe in it. If someone puts a sword to your throat and threatens to kill you, the fact that you don't believe in swords won't change reality. God's Word is likened to a sharp, two-edged sword, so keep on using it to cut to the heart, no matter what people say they believe. John Wesley said, "It is the ordinary method of the Spirit of God to convict sinners by the Law. It is this which, being set home on the conscience, generally breaks the rocks in pieces. It is more especially this part of the Word of God which is quick and powerful, full of life and energy and sharper than any two-edged sword."

TICK ...

TICK ...

TICK ...

TICK ...

TICK ...

TICK ...

TICK ...

TICK ...

TICK ...

TICK ...

TICK ...

TICK ...

TICK ...

**There goes another minute.
Gone forever. Go share your faith
while you still have time.**

TICK ...

TICK ...

TICK ...

TICK ...

TICK ...

TICK ...

TICK ...

TICK ...

180

The Deception of Idolatry

It seems that few in the civilized world believe in idols. But there is a subtle form of idolatry that deceives millions. It's the sin of creating a god to suit ourselves. We form an idol in the imagination of our minds, making our own *image* of God. The reason this is so popular is that "our" own god has no moral dictates. We pray to him, but he doesn't answer us, and worshippers of dumb idles love to have it so. That god wouldn't create Hell. He doesn't have a Moral Law or a Judgment Day. Such delusions give a "false peace." But there is an answer. George Whitefield said, "First, then, before you can speak peace to your hearts, you must be made to see, made to feel, made to weep over, made to bewail your actual transgressions against the Law of God."

There goes another minute.
Gone forever. Go share your faith
while you still have time.

TICK ...
TICK ...
TICK ...
TICK ...
TICK ...
TICK ...
TICK ...
TICK ...
TICK ...
TICK ...
TICK ...
TICK ...
TICK ...
TICK ...
TICK ...
TICK ...
TICK ...
TICK ...
TICK ...
TICK ...
TICK ...
TICK ...
TICK ...
TICK ...
TICK ...

181

Striving to be Happy

What do you want to achieve in this life? Most just want to be happy. But the problem with striving to be happy is that happiness is something for which we are forever striving. Rather, as Christians, we should aim for a higher goal. We should aim to be faithful to God, to hear the words, "Well done, you good and faithful servant." And if we serve God with a faithful heart, despite life's trials, we will achieve our life's goal. In the world's eyes, Jesus didn't do that. He ended up being crucified for His ideals. But we know differently. He was aiming at the resurrection. That made all the difference. That's what Paul aimed at in life. He said, "If, by any means, I may attain to the resurrection from the dead." [67] He was faithful to the end. We must be the same.

There goes another minute.
Gone forever. **Go share your faith while you still have time.**

God's Goodness

Until God gives us light, we have a darkened understanding of what is meant by His "goodness." In our ignorance, we think that if God is good, He would never create a place called Hell. Yet, the opposite is the case. If God is good, He must see to it that justice is done. No judge could be called "good" if he turned a blind eye to rape and murder. If he is good, he must do everything within his power to see that justice is done. It was C. S. Lewis who said, "When we merely say that we are bad, the 'wrath' of God seems a barbarous doctrine; as soon as we *perceive* our bad-ness, it appears inevitable, a mere corollary from God's goodness." In other words, once we see our sins under the light of God's holy standard, then judgment is unavoidable.

There goes another minute.
Gone forever. Go share your faith
while you still have time.

TICK ...
TICK ...
TICK ...
TICK ...
TICK ...
TICK ...
TICK ...
TICK ...
TICK ...
TICK ...
TICK ...
TICK ...
TICK ...
TICK ...
TICK ...
TICK ...
TICK ...
TICK ...
TICK ...
TICK ...
TICK ...
TICK ...
TICK ...
TICK ...
TICK ...
TICK ...

The Skydiving Voucher

A friend once said to his wife, "I'd like to one day try sky-diving." She didn't know that he was simply trying to impress her, and she secretly purchased a skydiving voucher for his birthday. The day he took his first plunge, he was terrified, but the day he first preached in the open air, he was just as terrified. Does the thought of open air preaching terrify you? Are you saying, "I could never do that!"? Be careful, because that's the qualification you need to do it. God wants people who have no ability. This was the case with Gideon, Moses, Jeremiah, Paul, and a host of others who said, "I could never do that!" ... but with the help of God, did it anyway. So, don't use inability as an excuse. See it as an asset. Take the plunge despite the terror.

There goes another minute.
Gone forever. Go share your faith
while you still have time.

Living For Him

The Bible says, "If any man love not the Lord Jesus Christ, let him be Anathema."[68] That means that if you don't love the Savior, you will be cursed forever. Do you love Him? Are you living for Him or for yourself? Have seen your sinful heart? Have you then seen the cross and understood that it was love for you that held Him there? Then you cannot help but love Him. He shed His blood so that the love of God could be shed abroad in our hearts. So the very least we can do for Him is to return that love by doing His will. And His will is to reach the lost. He said, "Go into all the world and preach the Gospel to every creature." All around you people are dying. Time is short. What are you waiting for?

There goes another minute.
Gone forever. Go share your faith
while you still have time.

Eating Habits

A thirty-year study of eating habits found that the vast majority of people end up grossly overweight. The researchers' conclusion was that we should never give up on dieting. How much better it is to rather have the virtue of self control, and so prevent the weight-gain in the first place. The Bible says that it would be better to put a knife to your throat than to be "given to appetite." The world is like the town that had a road that forced cars to drive around a bend and go over a cliff. The townspeople thought that they solved the problem by building a hospital at the bottom of the cliff. Wisdom would instead have put a guardrail at the top. A fence is always better than a funeral. We have a message that puts a fence between humanity and Hell. The blood of Jesus Christ prevents eternal damnation.

There goes another minute.
Gone forever. **Go share your faith while you still have time.**

The Proposal

A man from Florida decided to propose to his girlfriend in the moonlight of a Brazilian beach. Around midnight, the moon suddenly broke through the clouds, and he slipped the ring onto her finger. At that very moment, local fireworks appropriately exploded, and she accepted his proposal. He then told her a secret he had deliberately kept from her. He was a millionaire. When we first come to the Savior, we come to Him in His absolute poverty. He hangs before us, naked, on a cruel cross. We come as poverty-stricken and wretched sinners, hoping for reconciliation with a God we have greatly offended. It's only when we are forgiven that we begin to understand the unspeakable wealth we have in Christ ... wealth that makes all the riches of this world combined seem like the leftovers of a trash bin after it's been emptied.

There goes another minute.
Gone forever. Go share your faith
while you still have time.

No Fruit for Your Labor

Do you ever share your faith and see little or no fruit for your labors? You long to see at least one person come to Christ. If it hasn't yet happened, don't let discouragement quench your zeal. A hen will scratch harder when worms are scarce. If souls are scarce, pray more, witness more, and you will get your worms … if you don't give up. The Bible promises that they that sow in tears *shall* reap in joy. If you don't reap from your labors in this life, you will certainly reap in the next. John Wesley said to his preachers, "You have nothing to do but to win souls; therefore spend and be spent in this work." Spend your time planting the seed of the Word of God in the hearts of men and women, and God will bring fruit in His time.

**There goes another minute.
Gone forever. Go share your faith
while you still have time.**

The Lifeline to God

Prayer is our lifeline to God, and it is evident
that He is calling His Church to prayer. It is
the kind of prayer that will storm the gates of
Hell in the spirit realm. We need worldwide
revival in the Church that will boil over into
the whole wide world! We need to look at the
things that are not seen, and follow in the
footsteps of Abraham, who "staggered not at
the promise of God, but was strong in faith,
giving glory to God, being fully persuaded that
what God had promised, He was able to
perform."[69] Revival is God's will. He is not
willing that any perish; He wants *all* to "come
to a knowledge of the truth."[70] Therefore, we
can confidently pursue God for men, and then,
in urgent zeal, pursue men for God.

There goes another minute.
Gone forever. **Go share your faith
while you still have time.**

TICK ...
TICK ...
TICK ...
TICK ...
TICK ...
TICK ...
TICK ...
TICK ...
TICK ...
TICK ...
TICK ...
TICK ...
TICK ...
TICK ...
TICK ...
TICK ...
TICK ...
TICK ...
TICK ...
TICK ...
TICK ...
TICK ...
TICK ...
TICK ...
TICK ...
TICK ...
TICK ...
TICK ...

The Ignition of Prayer

Prayer was the ignition to every revival fire in history. It *was* and *is* the key to the door of ministry for every preacher used by God. For the soldier of Christ, true prayer should be a way of life, not just a call for help in the heat of battle. We are told to be "Praying always ... ," to "Continue in prayer ... " and to "Pray without ceasing"[71] Hudson Taylor, the great missionary, said, "The prayer power has never been tried to its full capacity. If we want to see mighty works of Divine power and grace wrought in the place of weakness, failure and disappointment, let us answer God's standing challenge, 'Call to me, and I will answer you, and show you great and mighty things, which you do not know.'" Seek God for men, and then seek men for God.

**There goes another minute.
Gone forever. Go share your faith
while you still have time.**

Holiness and Power

Holiness goes hand in hand with the word, "power." Jesus was "declared to be the Son of God with power, according to the Spirit of Holiness ... "[72] According to *Vine's Expository Dictionary*, "holiness" signifies a "separation to God, and the conduct befitting those so separated." This was the message preached by the early Church. They preached the great truth: "Without holiness, no man shall see the Lord."[73] They proclaimed, "Let everyone who names the name of Christ, depart from iniquity."[74] To live in holiness means to walk in the steps of Jesus ... in that same Spirit of Holiness. Leonard Ravenhill said, "Let no man think of fighting Hell's legions if he is still fighting an internal warfare. Carnage without will sicken him if he has carnality within. It is the man who has surrendered to the Lord who will never surrender to his enemies."

There goes another minute.
Gone forever. Go share your faith
while you still have time.

The Intimacy of Prayer

God loves His children coming to Him in the intimacy of prayer. The Scriptures tell us, "The prayer of the upright is His delight."[75] Do you want to delight God? Then be upright in Christ, and seek Him in prayer. As soldiers of Christ, we should never face a day in battle until we have faced the Father in prayer. John Bunyan said, "Prayer is a shield to the soul, a delight to God, and a scourge to Satan." Someone once said that Satan trembles when he sees the feeblest Christian on his knees. He flees when we resist him *if we are submitted to God*. Martin Luther said, "I have so much to do (today) that I should spend the first three hours in prayer." Maybe you don't have the time to go and spend the first three hours of each day in prayer, but at least pray as you go.

**There goes another minute.
Gone forever. Go share your faith
while you still have time.**

Driven to His Knees

The Apostle Paul had a deep concern for the lost. He had a love for the unsaved that drove him to his knees and then to stand up and witness of his faith. And he did so even in prison. Can you imagine the boldness you would need to witness to Roman guards, to men who were hardened to cruelty? Yet, Paul begged, "Pray for me, that utterance may be given to me, that I may open my mouth boldly to make known the mystery of the Gospel, for which I am an ambassador in chains; that in it I may speak boldly, as I ought to speak."[76] Instead of the attitude, "Oh no, here I am chained to two guards," his was, "Thank you Lord, I have two guards chained to me." We aren't in chains, so we must take advantage of the freedom we have to share our faith.

There goes another minute.
Gone forever. Go share your faith
while you still have time.

TICK ...
TICK ...
TICK ...
TICK ...
TICK ...
TICK ...
TICK ...
TICK ...
TICK ...
TICK ...
TICK ...
TICK ...
TICK ...
TICK ...
TICK ...
TICK ...
TICK ...
TICK ...
TICK ...
TICK ...
TICK ...
TICK ...
TICK ...
TICK ...
TICK ...
TICK ...
TICK ...
TICK ...
TICK ...

193

Whoever is Fearful

When God spoke to Gideon regarding the size of his army, He said, "Now therefore, proclaim in the hearing of the people, saying, 'Whoever is fearful and afraid, let him turn and depart at once from Mount Gilead.'"[77] God wants those who have overcome fear by being dead to themselves. He wants soldiers that have been crucified with Christ. George Mueller said, "There was a day when I died, utterly died, died to George Mueller, his opinions, preferences, tastes, and will—died to the world, its approval or censure—died to the approval or blame even of my brethren and friends—and since then I have only to show myself approved to God." The way to see if you are dead is to see how you react when God wants you to witness to an unsaved person. Are we dead to the whisperings of fear?

There goes another minute.
Gone forever. **Go share your faith while you still have time.**

Faith-filled Words

Caleb had given everything of himself to God. At the age of 85, he said, "As yet I am as strong this day as I was on the day that Moses sent me; just as my strength was then, so now is my strength for war, both for going out and for coming in."[78] Faith grows with experience. Look at his faith-filled words: "Now therefore, give me this mountain of which the Lord spoke in that day; for you heard in that day how the Anakims were there, and that the cities were great and fortified. It may be that the Lord will be with me, and I shall be able to drive them out as the Lord said."[79] Fighting the battle to reach the lost may seem like a mountainous task, but it is one that we can conquer through that same faith in God.

There goes another minute.
Gone forever. Go share your faith
while you still have time.

TICK...
TICK...
TICK...
TICK...
TICK...
TICK...
TICK...
TICK...
TICK...
TICK...
TICK...
TICK...
TICK...
TICK...
TICK...
TICK...
TICK...
TICK...
TICK...
TICK...
TICK...
TICK...
TICK...
TICK...
TICK...
TICK...

195

The Heavenly Rest

There is no such thing as an honorable discharge in the Army of God. Neither is there any such thing as retirement. The only retirement we will have is our promotion to Headquarters, as we pass from this life. Until that time, we must work while we have the opportunity and the inclination. Think of the words of the famous song, "American Pie." In the middle they are repeated — "This could be the day that I die ... this could be the day that I die." The Christian must remember that this could be his last day on earth. But while we may labor for the Lord, the Bible says that there is a special rest in which we have already entered. We entered that place of rest from our labors the moment we laid down trusted Him alone for our salvation.

There goes another minute.
Gone forever. Go share your faith
while you still have time.

Salt and Light

It is time for the Church to stand up in newfound courage, not only to *defend* ourselves, but to *attack* the enemy. We can so easily become distracted in a tangent of social work, and ignore the task of evangelism. But we are told to be salt *and* light. Salt has the ability to preserve and light shows the way in the darkness. We should not have one without the other. Certainly, we must speak up about issues such as abortion and other important moral issues. But to refrain from preaching the Gospel is to point to the wound without supplying the cure. The Bible says, "And have no fellowship with the unfruitful works of darkness, but rather expose them."[80] And the way to expose them is to preach the light of the glorious Gospel of Christ. The time to do that is now.

There goes another minute.
Gone forever. **Go share your faith while you still have time.**

I Am Full of the Matter

When Job was covered with sore boils, he had two "comforters" feed him lies. As Elihu listened, he said, "For I am full of the matter; the Spirit within me constrains me. Behold, my belly is like wine which has no vent. It is ready to burst, like new wine skins!"[81] When we look at the lies being fed to the Job of this world, as it sits covered in sore boils from head to foot, do we have Elihu's affirmation? Does a holy anger burn within us as the father of lies deceives this sick world? Does the Spirit of Truth live in us? Are we filled to a point where we cry, "The Spirit within me constrains me, pushes me on; the love of Christ burns within me! Behold my spirit is like wine which has no vent; it is ready to burst like new wine skins?"

There goes another minute. *Gone forever.* Go share your faith while you still have time.

Rock Your Cradle

If you are a sleeping saint, Satan will gladly rock your cradle. Oh, for a strong-sounding trumpet blast in the ear of those who would sleep — "Awake, awake, put on strength, O Zion … " If we sleep on our own domain, it won't be long before we are asleep on enemy territory. He will take what we don't defend. We haven't moved; it's just that the ground we are on has become occupied. Statistics tell us that only a tiny portion of the professed Body of Christ regularly shares their faith with others. People are going to Hell, and those who profess to love them don't have concern enough to warn them. Some of our churches are so dead, the only thing keeping many awake is the sound of snoring. Let's not only seek the lost, but pray that the Church would wake up to its great responsibility.

There goes another minute.
Gone forever. Go share your faith
while you still have time.

TICK ...
TICK ...
TICK ...
TICK ...
TICK ...
TICK ...
TICK ...
TICK ...
TICK ...
TICK ...

199

What Are You Doing?

What are you doing for the Kingdom of God? Have you taken the Great Commission to heart? Have you gone into all the world to preach the Gospel to every creature? Or are you waiting for a "word from God?" Then here it is— "Go." That's the first word of the Great Commission given to the Church 2000 years ago.[82] So, what are you waiting for? There's your word from God. Go somewhere; do something; say something to somebody somewhere, somehow. Someday you will be dead, and then it will be too late. While you can ... think, speak, move your hands and feet, do something for God. Are you content to sit in the barracks while the battle rages? You are in a battle for the lost. Form a platoon. Give out tracts everywhere, leave them somewhere, speak for your God. Don't be afraid of failure. Be afraid of silence.

There goes another minute.
Gone forever. **Go share your faith while you still have time.**

How Many Sermons?

There is no neutral ground in the battle for the souls of men and women. We are either gathering or we are scattering for the Kingdom of God. We have been given our clear battle orders. He who reads them cannot but hear the "sound of the trumpet, the alarm of war."[83] How many sermons do we have to take in before we give out? The average 12 year-old Christian has listened to close to 1,800 sermons. How many do you think you have listened to? Have they been sermons that exhort you to do the will of God and reach out to the lost? If not, take the initiative … "Preach the word! Be ready in season and out of season. Convince, rebuke, exhort, with all longsuffering and teaching … do the work of an evangelist, fulfill your ministry."[84]

There goes another minute.
Gone forever. Go share your faith
while you still have time.

TICK ...
TICK ...
TICK ...
TICK ...
TICK ...
TICK ...
TICK ...
TICK ...
TICK ...
TICK ...
TICK ...
TICK ...
TICK ...
TICK ...
TICK ...
TICK ...
TICK ...
TICK ...
TICK ...
TICK ...
TICK ...
TICK ...
TICK ...
TICK ...
TICK ...
TICK ...
TICK ...
TICK ...

201

Two Dates on the Calendar

Martin Luther said, "I only have two dates on my calendar—today and Judgment Day." How wise it is to live for those two days. While Judgment is probably the last thing on the mind of the world, it should be the first thing on the mind of the Christian because such a thought should help him walk in the fear of the Lord. It will help him keep his heart free from sin. But more than that, it will horrify him when he sees this world soak up sin as though there were no tomorrow. This world's love for iniquity justifies God's wrath. Think of their fate: "... but to those who are self-seeking and do not obey the truth, but obey unrighteousness indignation and wrath, tribulation and anguish, on every soul of man who does evil, of the Jew first and also of the Greek."[85]

There goes another minute. *Gone forever.* Go share your faith while you still have time.

202

The Radical Experience

Do you remember the first time you were born?
It was a radical experience. You didn't exist; then
suddenly you did. God gave you life. Being
born again is just as radical. One moment you
had no concern for God, and then suddenly you
were a new creature in Christ. You had a carnal
mind that was at enmity with God and your
understanding darkened. You were an enemy
of God in your mind through wicked works,
and even your thoughts were an abomination
to the Lord.[86] But upon conversion, God put
His Law into your mind,[87] giving you a new
mind—the "mind of Christ," and renewing you
in the "spirit" of your mind. Now your
thoughts are different. Now you have a mind
to do His will, and His will is for you to seek
the lost.

There goes another minute.
Gone forever. Go share your faith
while you still have time.

God's Thoughts

The Bible is unique, because in it we see God Himself speaking to humanity. In Isaiah 55:6-8, the prophet says, "Seek the Lord while He may be found, call upon Him while He is near." Then God Himself speaks to humanity: "For My thoughts are not your thoughts, neither are your ways My ways, says the Lord." In the Old Testament, God spoke to us through the prophets. In the New Testament, He spoke to us through His Son. And never did God speak so clearly as at the cross. In it, He expressed His great love for humanity. In it, He provided salvation for a lost and dying world. Now we can tell this world to seek the Lord while He may be found. Now we can tell them that through the new birth, God's thoughts can be our thoughts, and His ways can be our ways.

There goes another minute.
Gone forever. **Go share your faith while you still have time.**

TICK ...
TICK ...
TICK ...
TICK ...
TICK ...
TICK ...
TICK ...
TICK ...
TICK ...
TICK ...
TICK ...
TICK ...
TICK ...
TICK ...
TICK ...
TICK ...
TICK ...
TICK ...
TICK ...
TICK ...
TICK ...
TICK ...
TICK ...
TICK ...
TICK ...
TICK ...
TICK ...
TICK ...

The Original Greek

You may not be aware that the original Greek meaning of "The Great Commission." If you study the words, "Go into all the world and preach the Gospel to every creature,"[88] a whole new world of interesting thoughts opens up. According to the text, the Greek word for "go" is very fascinating. It is *poreuomai*, meaning, "go." The word "all" also carries with it intriguing connotations. It is *hapas*, and actually means "all." And if that doesn't rivet you, look closely at the word "every." It is *pas*, and literally means "every." So when Jesus said, "Go into all the world and preach the Gospel to every creature," to be true and faithful to the original text, what He was actually saying was, "Go into all the world and preach the Gospel to every creature." We are so fortunate to have access to such knowledge.

There goes another minute.
Gone forever. **Go share your faith while you still have time.**

TICK ...
TICK ...
TICK ...
TICK ...
TICK ...
TICK ...
TICK ...
TICK ...
TICK ...
TICK ...
TICK ...
TICK ...
TICK ...
TICK ...
TICK ...
TICK ...
TICK ...
TICK ...
TICK ...
TICK ...
TICK ...
TICK ...
TICK ...
TICK ...
TICK ...

205

The Will of God

What is the will of God for your life? Those who, like John, lay their head on the breast of Jesus will know His heartbeat. His will is very clear to those who have a close relationship with Him. If we don't know His will, Ephesians 5:17 says that we are unwise—"Therefore do not be unwise, but understand what the will of the Lord is." The Apostle Paul's prayer for the believer was that he would be "filled with the knowledge of His will."[89] The very reason God came to this earth in the person of Jesus Christ and suffered on the cross was for the salvation of the world. Has God lost His enthusiasm to see the lost saved? Has He changed His mind and is He now willing for sinners to perish? No, His will is that none perish, and that all come to repentance.

**There goes another minute.
Gone forever. Go share your faith
while you still have time.**

This Same Jesus

When Jesus ascended into Heaven, it must have been a glorious sight. The angels said to the disciples, "... this same Jesus will come in like manner."[90] He ascended in the same manner in which He will come! Therefore, there must have been "clouds, power and great glory." When the disciples were caught up in the glory of the ascension, the two angels appeared and brought them back to this world with the words, "Men of Galilee, why do you stand gazing up into Heaven?"[91] The inference was, "Don't stand here gazing up into the heavens. God has granted everlasting life to sinful humanity. Go and wait for the power to take the Gospel to the world." We haven't been saved to gaze up to Heaven, but to take the light to those who sit in the dark shadow of death.

There goes another minute.
Gone forever. Go share your faith
while you still have time.

TICK ...
TICK ...
TICK ...
TICK ...
TICK ...
TICK ...
TICK ...
TICK ...
TICK ...
TICK ...
TICK ...
TICK ...
TICK ...
TICK ...
TICK ...
TICK ...
TICK ...
TICK ...
TICK ...
TICK ...
TICK ...
TICK ...
TICK ...
TICK ...
TICK ...
TICK ...

207

Would We Step Up the Program?

When John Wesley was asked what he would do with his life if he knew that he would die at midnight the next day, his answer was something like this: "I would just carry on with what I am doing. I will arise at 5:00 a.m. for prayer, then take a house meeting at 6.00 a.m. At 12 noon, I will be preaching at an open-air. At 3:00 p.m. I have another meeting in another town. At 6:00 p.m. I have a house meeting. At 10:00 p.m. I have a prayer meeting and at 12:00 midnight, I would go to be with my Lord." If we knew we were to die at 12 o'clock tomorrow night, would we have to step up our evangelistic program? Hopefully, we are so on fire for God that we would just carry on as we are.

There goes another minute.
Gone forever. Go share your faith
while you still have time.

The Backbone

It would seem that there are only three types of people in this world—the jawbone, the wishbone, and the backbone. The jawbone says he will do something for God one day. He never puts his muscle where his mouth is. He prays about things, but never does them. The wishbone gazes with starry eyes at his godly heroes and wishes he could be like them. His is a world of dreams. He wishes he could preach, write, pray, sing and dance. Yet, no one ever did anything without doing something. An aspiration will only become a realization with perspiration. If he wants to see revival, he should stop wishing and start fishing, but his dreams are not fuel enough to motivate him. But the backbone sees Goliath and runs toward him. He leaves the fat cat of indifference sleeping by the fire.

There goes another minute.
Gone forever. Go share your faith
while you still have time.

TICK ...
TICK ...
TICK ...
TICK ...
TICK ...
TICK ...
TICK ...
TICK ...
TICK ...
TICK ...
TICK ...
TICK ...
TICK ...
TICK ...
TICK ...
TICK ...
TICK ...
TICK ...
TICK ...
TICK ...
TICK ...
TICK ...
TICK ...
TICK ...
TICK ...
TICK ...
TICK ...
TICK ...

209

Taught How to Live

Treat every minute of your time as though it was your last, because one day it will be. Remind yourself of that scary fact at the break of every day. A great preacher said we can be taught to live by remembering that we have to die. Always remember that the wisest thing you can do with time is to seek and save the lost. You have to *seek* them. Rarely will they come to you. When you talk to them, be as gentle as a dove and as stubborn as a mule. Be loving, kind, gentle, but obstinately uncompromising when it comes to the issue of sin. Tell them that the Moral Law will be God's standard on Judgment Day, and that God isn't willing for them to perish. Then preach the incredible love of God in Christ.

**There goes another minute.
Gone forever. Go share your faith
while you still have time.**

The Vast Army

Have you ever seen someone react to the Ten Commandments with the "deer in the headlights" look? They realize that they have sinned against God and that there's no escape. That's the look of *conviction*. That, more than likely, means they are ready for the Gospel. The Law prepares the heart for grace. This is how Jesus used the Law. So imitate Him, and never underestimate your contribution to the Kingdom of God. Even though you may sometimes feel alone, you are part of a vast army who are all fighting for the salvation of this dying world. So, be a good soldier of Jesus Christ and fight the good fight of faith. Do all you can to be the best you can to reach as many as you can. And the best way to do that is to simply ask, "What did Jesus do?" And then do what Jesus did.

There goes another minute.
Gone forever. **Go share your faith while you still have time.**

TICK ...
TICK ...
TICK ...
TICK ...
TICK ...
TICK ...
TICK ...
TICK ...
TICK ...
TICK ...
TICK ...
TICK ...
TICK ...
TICK ...
TICK ...
TICK ...
TICK ...
TICK ...
TICK ...
TICK ...
TICK ...
TICK ...
TICK ...
TICK ...
TICK ...
TICK ...
TICK ...

On What Will You Focus?

Do you care about the lost? Then think of yourself as a doctor who has a patient with a terminal disease. He must be treated immediately or he will die. You have a cure for him. So, what are you going to do—chat about the weather? No. Your focus is on the cure you have for him. You therefore swing the conversation the way you want it to go. You lovingly and deliberately take control. This is what Jesus did in John chapter 4. He went from water to God. You could swing to the things of God by offering a tract and saying, "It's a Gospel tract. Have you had a Christian background?" Or you could gently ask, "Do you ever think about what's going to happen to you after you die?" Whatever you do, do something ... and do it today.

There goes another minute. *Gone forever*. Go share your faith while you still have time.

Think of the Ant

The Bible says to consider the ant. It's not much bigger than a pinhead. Consider its little brain. It instinctively tells him what to do. He has work to do, and he does it each day. He has eyes, tiny legs, skin, a little heart, blood, and blood vessels to carry oxygen to his tiny lungs and nutrients throughout his body. He sleeps at night and arises the next day with an instinct to work. How could God create an ant that does all that? How could He not only fashion him to do what he does, but even know what the ant is thinking? And yet, the ant is just a tiny part of this incredible creation of God. How great is our Creator. And this same God commands us to preach His Gospel to every creature, and even promises to go with us.

There goes another minute.
Gone forever. Go share your faith
while you still have time.

TICK ...
TICK ...
TICK ...
TICK ...
TICK ...
TICK ...
TICK ...
TICK ...

Open the Veil

The Bible says of the Apostle Paul, that when he persuaded his hearers concerning Jesus from "the Law of Moses," he *solemnly* testified. The solemn use of the Law was second nature to Paul. He was brought up at the feet of Gamaliel, the great teacher of the Law, and was "taught according to the perfect manner of the law of the fathers ... "[92] He regularly used it to humble those who transgressed its holy precepts by pulling back the veil of Moses so that his hearers could have the light of the knowledge of the glory of God in the face of Jesus Christ. William Tyndale said, "Expound the Law truly and open the veil of Moses to condemn all flesh and prove all men sinners, and set at broach the mercy of our Lord Jesus, and let the wounded consciences drink of Him."

There goes another minute.
Gone forever. Go share your faith
while you still have time.

Lower the Law

Do you ever do what Jesus did and use the Ten Commandments to show sinners that they need a Savior? That's the Commandments' purpose—to bring to the knowledge of sin. Listen to what Charles Spurgeon said of the Law: "Lower the Law and you dim the light by which man perceives his guilt; this is a very serious loss to the sinner rather than a gain; for it lessens the likelihood of his conviction and conversion. I say you have deprived the Gospel of its ablest auxiliary [its most powerful weapon] when you have set aside the Law. You have taken away from it the schoolmaster that is to bring men to Christ ... They will never accept grace till they tremble before a just and holy Law. Therefore the Law serves a most necessary purpose, and it must not be removed from its place."

There goes another minute.
Gone forever. **Go share your faith while you still have time.**

Who's Stirring the Hornets

Have you ever had anyone try to discourage you from using the Law to show sinners that they need a Savior? Why would anyone oppose it when, in fact, Jesus used it? Martin Luther put his finger on why. In a sermon in which he spoke of the Law being used as a schoolmaster to bring sinners to Christ, he shows *who it is* that stirs up the hornet's nest. He gave these words of warning: "This now is the Christian teaching and preaching, which God be praised, we know and possess, and it is not necessary at present to develop it further, but only to offer the admonition that it be maintained in Christendom with all diligence. *For Satan has attacked it hard and strong from the beginning until the present, and gladly would he completely extinguish it and tread it underfoot.*"

There goes another minute. *Gone forever*. Go share your faith while you still have time.

Consider Nathan

Consider how Nathan the Prophet approached King David after he sinned with Bathsheba. He said that the king had despised the Commandment of the Lord, that he had done evil in the sight of God. He said that he had committed murder and adultery, and then the preacher boldly pronounced stinging judgment upon the king. But look at the wonderful result of Nathan's faithfulness to God: "David said to Nathan, 'I have sinned against the Lord.'"[93] If we preach a message that doesn't cut deep into the sinner's conscience, we may fill our churches, but they will be filled with people who don't see that they have *sinned against the Lord*, and if there's no repentance, there is no salvation. So, don't hold back. Make sure you faithfully preach the truth in love, and do it today.

**There goes another minute.
Gone forever. Go share your faith
while you still have time.**

TICK ...
TICK ...
TICK ...
TICK ...
TICK ...
TICK ...
TICK ...
TICK ...
TICK ...
TICK ...
TICK ...
TICK ...
TICK ...
TICK ...
TICK ...
TICK ...
TICK ...
TICK ...
TICK ...
TICK ...
TICK ...
TICK ...
TICK ...
TICK ...
TICK ...
TICK ...
TICK ...
TICK ...
TICK ...

Consumed By His Anger

The Bible says, "For we are consumed by your anger, and by your wrath are we troubled. You have set our iniquities before you, our secret sins in the light of your countenance."[94] The world isn't "troubled" by God's wrath. They are offended by the thought that He is angry at them. Nevertheless, the Bible says that they are "consumed" by His anger. It abides on them and envelopes them as a raging fire. This is because He has set their iniquities in front of Him, like a judge who places all the evidence of a heinous crime on the bench before him before he passes sentence. But more than that, their *secret* sins are in the light of His countenance. They are not at His feet. They are in front of His face. He sees every wicked thought and deed. No wonder Paul said, "Wherefore knowing the terror of the Lord, we persuade men."[95]

**There goes another minute.
Gone forever. Go share your faith
while you still have time.**

The Continual Feast

God gave this world life. Yet, they use His name to cuss. He gave them the ability to see, to hear, to think; yet they don't think, see, or hear. They are willfully blind, deaf, and dumb. They act like an angry and dumb dog who bites the owner who gave him his food. But the Christian is no longer dumb. The eyes of His understanding have been enlightened by the grace of our God. He can now see that every good and perfect gift comes down from the Father of Lights. He is filled with thanksgiving to God not only for the gift of life, but for the incredible display of love seen at the cross. He has food to eat of which this godless world knows nothing. The cross gives him a merry heart and a continual feast. This is the food that keeps him energized to do the will of God.

There goes another minute.
Gone forever. Go share your faith
while you still have time.

Full Surrender

George Whitefield said, "I had a day in my life when I fully surrendered in consecration to the Lord and that day I said, 'I call Heaven and earth to witness that I give up myself entirely to be a martyr for Him who hung on the cross for me. I have thrown myself blind-folded and without reserve into His mighty hands!'" He surrendered his everything, because Jesus surrendered everything at the cross. The soldier of the Christ, who has seen God's commendation of the love towards him, cannot help but fling himself into the heat of the battle, constrained by the same irresistible force that drove Jesus to Calvary. The Savior went to the cross because He loved God and man. Prove your love for God by loving humanity enough to warn them of the reality of Hell ... and of their need of the Savior.

There goes another minute.
Gone forever. Go share your faith
while you still have time.

They Cannot Pass

John Bunyan said that it will be the Law that will damn sinners from Heaven. He warned, "And, indeed, this Law is the flaming sword that turns every way; yes, that lies to this day in the way to Heaven, for a bar to all unbelievers and unsanctified professors … " They *cannot* bypass the sword that flames with the burning heat of perfect and eternal justice. It moves its sharp and fiery blade at lightning speed to cut down all who transgress its perfect precepts. As the Scriptures say, it will make sure that "every transgression … will receive a just recompense of reward."[96] We must never forget that that sword fell on the Savior so that we could pass by its razor-sharp blade. Now we can serve Him in reverence and godly fear.[97]

There goes another minute.
Gone forever. Go share your faith
while you still have time.

TICK ...
TICK ...
TICK ...
TICK ...
TICK ...
TICK ...
TICK ...
TICK ...
TICK ...
TICK ...
TICK ...
TICK ...
TICK ...
TICK ...
TICK ...
TICK ...
TICK ...
TICK ...
TICK ...
TICK ...
TICK ...
TICK ...
TICK ...
TICK ...
TICK ...
TICK ...
TICK ...

Helping the Butterfly

A man once noticed that a butterfly was struggling to get out of a cocoon, so he took a razor blade and slit the side of it to help the poor creature. It struggled, then fell out onto the ground, and after a little movement, died. The man hadn't helped the butterfly; he had killed it. The very process of struggling in the cocoon should have pumped blood into the wings of the butterfly, giving it beauty, life, and character. In the same way, all the trials and struggling which come our way are not to do us harm, but to do us good. They are bringing beauty and color to our character, which will be revealed the moment we break free from the cocoon of this life. So, don't wait to be free from trials before you reach out to those who are still in the shadow of death.

There goes another minute. *Gone forever.* Go share your faith while you still have time.

Rejoice Anyway

If we have faith in God, we will keep our joy in our trials. It may be a matter of saying, "I don't know what's going on, but I will rejoice anyway, and give God thanks because all things are working together for my good." This isn't easy to do, but the Bible exhorts us to trust in the Lord with all our hearts, and lean not to our own understanding. A good athlete doesn't buckle under the pressure. He lets the pressure strengthen his muscles. The Psalmist said, "It is good for me that I have been afflicted, that I may learn Your statutes. I know, O Lord, that Your judgments are right, and that in faithfulness, You have afflicted me."[98] And proof that you truly trust God is that you will keep doing His will by reaching out to the unsaved while you are in affliction.

There goes another minute.
Gone forever. Go share your faith
while you still have time.

Thunder Can Help

When we understand the greatness, the majesty, the power, the magnificence, the glory, the nobility, the splendor, the grandeur, the supremacy, and the ability of our God, then we will begin to *really* fear Him. Thunder and lightning can help us do this. When the earth trembles with thunder, and lightning makes the darkness flee at the speed of light, we see a tiny display of the power of our God. Think of the sun. It's just a medium-sized star; yet, its energy and violence almost defy imagination. It is a dense mass of glowing matter—a million times the volume of the earth, in a permanent state of nuclear activity. This God who created all things requires an account of every word. Better to fall onto the surface of the sun than to fall into the hands of the Living God.

There goes another minute.
Gone forever. **Go share your faith while you still have time.**

Human Beings

The word, "human" means "lowly" and the word, "being," means "aware of existence." As human beings, we are lowly creatures made from the dust, and we are aware of our existence. It seems that we are the only ones in God's creation that have the knowledge of existence and our appointment with death. And from the very core of our existence, we cry, "Oh, I don't want to die!" That "will to live" is a strong consolation to Christians because we can appeal to it when we speak to the lost. We can remind them of that cry and ask them to listen to it, because if there was only one chance in a million that the Bible is right when it says that Jesus Christ has abolished death, they owe it to their good sense to open their hearts and at least listen to the claims of Scripture.

There goes another minute.
Gone forever. **Go share your faith while you still have time.**

The Ice-Cold Hand

When Jesus lay in the tomb, death laid its ice-cold hand upon His body. His heart sat like a cold rock within His breast. His cold fingers lay still and stiff. Suddenly, deep within the heart of the Son of God came a beat … one beat, the implications of which resounded blessed hope throughout the whole earth. Another heart beat followed, and then another. Within seconds, color began to return to the flesh of the Messiah. His stiffened fingers began to move. His chest raised as He breathed air into His still lungs. *Life broke the steel bands of death from the body of the Son of the Living God.* Just as four words from the mouth of the Creator had caused light to flood the universe in the beginning, so, in this new beginning, light had flooded the dark tomb. *It was not possible that death could hold Him!*[99]

There goes another minute. *Gone forever.* Go share your faith while you still have time.

TICK ...
TICK ...
TICK ...
TICK ...
TICK ...
TICK ...
TICK ...
TICK ...
TICK ...
TICK ...
TICK ...
TICK ...
TICK ...
TICK ...
TICK ...
TICK ...
TICK ...
TICK ...
TICK ...
TICK ...
TICK ...
TICK ...
TICK ...
TICK ...
TICK ...
TICK ...
TICK ...
TICK ...

The Empty Hand Grenade

For the Christian, death is but an empty hand grenade, a defused bomb, and a vacant threat. It is under our feet through faith in Jesus. It is but a dark door with a golden handle that opens to the pure and brilliant light of eternal joy. How tragic that the world doesn't know what we have found in Christ. We must tell them, but if the Lord tarries, we will find that old age will hinder us from doing exploits for God that are a breeze to the young. May He use our eyes to see the harvest while we can still see. May He use our ears to hear the cries of the lost while we can still hear. May He use our mouths to speak while we can still speak, our hands to reach out to the unsaved, and our feet to carry to them the Gospel of peace.

There goes another minute.
Gone forever. **Go share your faith**
while you still have time.

TICK ...
TICK ...
TICK ...
TICK ...
TICK ...
TICK ...
TICK ...
TICK ...
TICK ...
TICK ...
TICK ...
TICK ...
TICK ...
TICK ...
TICK ...
TICK ...
TICK ...
TICK ...
TICK ...
TICK ...
TICK ...
TICK ...
TICK ...
TICK ...
TICK ...
TICK ...

227

Waiting On Tables

The early Church had a shortage of people to wait on tables, so they *commissioned* people to do so. Stephen was one who was handpicked to wait on tables, but he couldn't remain serving within the confines of the Church. His fire couldn't be contained. He was full of the Holy Spirit. The Zeal of God's House had eaten him up. He had food to eat that most of us don't know. He *had* to preach in the open air. Nowadays we have many who kindly "wait on tables." Nowadays it is the Great Commission that is being neglected. May the fire of the Holy Spirit move on each of us and make us go open-air. Our Father's business is to seek and save the lost, and once we are on fire, we cannot confine our ministry to waiting on tables.

There goes another minute.
Gone forever. **Go share your faith**
while you still have time.

Fell From the Third Story

While Paul was preaching, a young man sat in a room where we are told there were many lights. Perhaps he was warmed by the fires that gave the room light. As he sat in a window, it neared midnight. Suddenly, sleep enveloped him and he fell from the third story and was killed. But Paul raised him from the dead, and carried on teaching. It is the midnight hour, and as we sit in the window of eternity, we can never allow sleep to overtake us. Even if the Christian life seems to be a dry and lifeless sermon without end, and the joy of feeding on God's Word is no longer in our hearts, we cannot let apathy overtake us. We must get on our knees and return to our first love. Then we must get on our feet and do what we have been saved for.

**There goes another minute.
Gone forever. Go share your faith
while you still have time.**

TICK ...
TICK ...
TICK ...
TICK ...
TICK ...
TICK ...
TICK ...
TICK ...
TICK ...
TICK ...
TICK ...
TICK ...
TICK ...
TICK ...
TICK ...
TICK ...
TICK ...
TICK ...
TICK ...
TICK ...
TICK ...
TICK ...
TICK ...
TICK ...
TICK ...
TICK ...
TICK ...
TICK ...

Written for the Humble

The Bible is a special book. It is written for the humble. Those proud hearts who are not born of the Spirit will understandably end up confused if they try to read it. The Chinese language sounds very complex and strange to those who don't speak it, yet a four-year old Chinese child can easily understand it, because he has been *born* into a Chinese family. The Chinese language is not darkness, but light to him. And the language of Scripture will be nothing but babble to those who are not *born* into the family of God. The Bible says, "The natural man receives not the things of the Spirit of God, neither can he know them, they are foolishness to him, because they are spiritually understood."[100] He must be born into the family of God, so that he can understand spiritual things.

There goes another minute.
Gone forever. **Go share your faith while you still have time.**

Slam Him Against the Wall

It's important to take a person professing to be an atheist through the Moral Law *before* you mention God. When you ask him if he has kept the Ten Commandments, you are not asking about his belief in God, or whether or not he thinks Hell exists. So initially, the subject of his beliefs probably won't arise. As you use the Law, you will be encouraged when you see what a powerful weapon God has given you. Every now and then, an unrelenting Law will slam a hardened rebel against the wall, frisk him for secret sins, and then point their ten great cannons at his face. You will see an actual change in his face as he feels the cold steel of the pistol of his own conscience against the warm flesh of his head. His mouth is stopped by the Law, and that prepares his heart to listen to his only hope of salvation.

**There goes another minute.
Gone forever. Go share your faith
while you still have time.**

TICK ...
TICK ...
TICK ...
TICK ...
TICK ...
TICK ...
TICK ...
TICK ...
TICK ...
TICK ...
TICK ...
TICK ...
TICK ...
TICK ...
TICK ...
TICK ...
TICK ...
TICK ...
TICK ...
TICK ...
TICK ...
TICK ...
TICK ...
TICK ...
TICK ...
TICK ...
TICK ...

231

Thoughts About the Brain

Do you ever give thought to your brain? It's an amazing piece of equipment. It's really just a chunk of meat weighing about four or five pounds. If you threw it to a hungry dog, he would probably eat it. Yet, not all the sophisticated computers in the world combined can do what this brain does. It can think on its own ... yours may be doing that right now. The brain is incredible. And yet dumb dogs and scrawny cats also have brains, and theirs, in some ways, are more sophisticated than ours. Can you catch a fast-moving Frisbee in your mouth, or always land on your feet if you are thrown in the air? Yet, there is an evident difference between the animals and us. God has placed eternity in our hearts. Let's use our God-given brains today and tap into eternity by seeking the lost.

There goes another minute.
Gone forever. **Go share your faith while you still have time.**

Caught Off Guard

Harry Houdini was the most famous escape artist to ever live. Even though he defied death so many times, he didn't die trying to escape from some death-defying feat. A young man, who had heard about Houdini's incredibly strong stomach muscles, approached him backstage and punched him in the stomach. Unfortunately, Houdini was caught off guard, received a ruptured appendix, and died seven days later of peritonitis. Satan knows that the Christian can sometimes be caught backstage, off guard. That's why there are so many warnings in Scripture about "watching" and being "sober and vigilant"—*because your adversary, the devil, walks about seeking whom he may strike in the stomach.* Each of us needs to have the strong and braced muscle of a holy lifestyle that can resist the blows of the devil. So always be ready, and in the meanwhile, carry on with your death-defying message.

**There goes another minute.
Gone forever. Go share your faith
while you still have time.**

TICK ...
TICK ...
TICK ...
TICK ...
TICK ...
TICK ...
TICK ...
TICK ...
TICK ...
TICK ...
TICK ...
TICK ...
TICK ...
TICK ...
TICK ...
TICK ...
TICK ...
TICK ...
TICK ...
TICK ...
TICK ...
TICK ...
TICK ...
TICK ...
TICK ...
TICK ...

Completely Sold Out

When you study the *Book of Acts,* you will see that the Church was on fire. The zeal of God's House had eaten them up. They were about their Father's business. They were whole-heartedly sold out for the Kingdom of God. That's the key to being effective in reaching the lost. The Bible says, " … the eyes of the Lord run to and fro throughout the whole earth, to show himself strong on behalf of them whose heart is perfect toward Him."[101] The word "perfect" simply means, "to be completely sold out to God." Many Christians are living in defeat because they are not serving God with that perfect heart, and so the Lord is not showing Himself strong on their behalf. Today, be sold out to God by reaching out to the unsaved, and watch Him show Himself strong on your behalf.

There goes another minute.
Gone forever. **Go share your faith**
while you still have time.

The Height for Your Neck

In the late 1970s, a 20 year-old man was on a snowmobile in Colfax, Iowa. He was racing around on the glistening, white snow, and sped between two wooden posts at about thirty miles an hour. That was the last thing he did. A thin, almost invisible wire between the posts decapitated him. Satan will let you race around, enjoying the pleasures of sin. But the pleasure is only for a season. If you are in his territory, you therefore give him permission to devour you. According to Jesus, his will is to "kill, steal and destroy,"[102] and somewhere he has a wire strung at just the right height for your neck. All he needs is a little cooperation. He wants you to put your foot on the accelerator and get up a little speed. Stay out of his playground. Keep your heart free of sin.

There goes another minute.
Gone forever. **Go share your faith while you still have time.**

TICK ...
TICK ...
TICK ...
TICK ...
TICK ...
TICK ...
TICK ...
TICK ...
TICK ...
TICK ...
TICK ...
TICK ...
TICK ...
TICK ...
TICK ...
TICK ...
TICK ...
TICK ...
TICK ...
TICK ...
TICK ...
TICK ...
TICK ...
TICK ...
TICK ...
TICK ...
TICK ...

235

The Ex-cat Burglar

A popular magazine once ran an article by an ex-cat burglar. He didn't steal cats; he preyed on the homes of those of us who are ignorant of his ways. Most of us may as well put up a sign saying, "Thieves, I'm out of town, so come in and steal what you want." We have unlit rear entrances, which are enshrouded by trees and hedges. They act as magnets for the burglar. The ex-thief said that a loud air conditioner was an open invitation. If people could sleep through its noise, they weren't going to hear him breaking into their home. The man's best advice to stop burglars: "Get two dogs, and make sure they bark." So, if you want to stop the thief that Jesus said came to kill, steal, and destroy, have the guard dog of a good conscience, and listen when he barks. He is there to protect you.

**There goes another minute.
Gone forever. Go share your faith
while you still have time.**

God's Fair Earth

Let's look at an average day on God's fair earth.
Perhaps today we will have a volcanic eruption
or an earthquake that will crush families to
death beneath the debris of their homes.
Cancerous diseases will continue to take their
toll and cause thousands to die in agony.
Multitudes will perish from fatal ailments that
have always plagued mankind, from asthma to
typhoid to leprosy to heart disease. Today,
human beings will be struck by lightning,
drowned in floods, stung to death by killer bees,
killed by hurricanes and tornadoes, and
tormented by blight, pestilence, and
infestations. They will be afflicted, devastated,
and brought to ruin. Maybe there is no God
(only a fool says that), or maybe God can't
control His creation, or maybe we live in a fallen
creation. Common sense tells us that we live in
a fallen creation. But thank God, we can be
lifted from the fall through the Gospel.

There goes another minute.
Gone forever. **Go share your faith**
while you still have time.

TICK ...
TICK ...
TICK ...
TICK ...
TICK ...
TICK ...
TICK ...
TICK ...
TICK ...
TICK ...
TICK ...
TICK ...
TICK ...
TICK ...
TICK ...
TICK ...
TICK ...
TICK ...
TICK ...
TICK ...
TICK ...
TICK ...
TICK ...
TICK ...
TICK ...
TICK ...
TICK ...
TICK ...

237

We Understand by Faith

The Christian is told that he *understands* "by faith." For instance, if we have major surgery, we trust the surgeon even though we have no real understanding of how he is going to operate on us. We have to trust him or there will be no operation. We understand that he has the ability to make us well, so we choose to have faith in him and his abilities. In the same manner, we trust God. Many have died at the hands of surgeons, but no one perishes who places himself or herself in the hands of God. His ability is boundless and His promises are "an anchor of the soul, both sure and steadfast."[103] Doctors and pilots will fail you, friends you trust will disappoint you, elevators will let you down, but the promises of Almighty God are utterly trustworthy.

There goes another minute.
Gone forever. Go share your faith
while you still have time.

Succulent Grapes

How wonderful God is to sinful man. Succulent grapes hang in a bunch waiting to be plucked by him. Pistachio nuts split their sides to let him know they are ready to be eaten. Apricots drip with a luscious liquid that makes his mouth water at the mere thought of them. Peaches blush on the tree to let him know that they are ready to be consumed. Heat from the sun transforms the lemon from green to yellow to tell him it's ready for those with a taste for tart. Oranges pile high in the supermarket stack, as hand-sized leak-free containers of a sweet, healthy liquid. Even when the wrapper is peeled away, each of the removable edible segments of juice is self-sealed and mouth-shaped. Add to all this the fact that He offers sinful man everlasting life through the glorious Gospel, and we catch of glimpse of how good God is.

There goes another minute.
Gone forever. **Go share your faith while you still have time.**

One Hundred Years Old

It's a fact of life that we could be dead tomorrow. But we find that so hard to believe. Death is something that happens to *other* people. In 1971, health author Jerome Rodale said, "I'm going to live to be one hundred." He died the next day at the age of fifty-one. But even if he had lived until he was a hundred years old, he would still have died. Someone once said, "There are only two things in life that are sure—death and taxes." That's not true. Plenty of people avoid taxes; nobody avoids death. Ten out of ten die. The leading actor of a popular TV series put it this way: "Death is a guarantee from the day we are born. But I guess we don't think about it because we think it will never happen." How right he was.

There goes another minute. *Gone forever.* Go share your faith while you still have time.

Power to Transform

The incredible thing about God's promise of eternal life is that He backs it up with His Holy Spirit to show us that He means what He says. Just as you could prove the reality of electricity by experiencing an electric shock, so God's promises carry a punch with them. If you refuse to believe in electricity, put a fork in an electrical outlet. Suddenly you will become a believer, because you have experienced the power. The Bible tells us that when the Gospel is preached, it comes "in power, and in the Holy Spirit and in much assurance."[104] What a joy it is to see that power transform someone and make him or her a brand new creature. God has a way of turning men like Saul of Tarsus into men like the Apostle Paul, who live only to reach the lost. We need more like that.

There goes another minute.
Gone forever. Go share your faith
while you still have time.

Law Work

Martyn Lloyd-Jones said, "The trouble with people who are not seeking for a Savior, and for salvation, is that they do not understand the nature of sin. It is the peculiar function of the Law to bring such an understanding to a man's mind and conscience. That is why great evangelical preachers 300 years ago in the time of the Puritans, and 200 years ago in the time of Whitefield and others, always engaged in what they called a preliminary 'Law work.'" Many involved in evangelism have neglected to prepare the soil with the Law before they sow the seed of the Gospel, and understandably, they reap a disappointing crop. Such unbiblical practice will have eternal and devastating repercussions. So, make sure you do what Jesus did. If someone is proud, use the Law to bring the knowledge of sin *before* you preach the Gospel.

There goes another minute. *Gone forever.* Go share your faith while you still have time.

Training for Battle

Trials strengthen the Christian and bring him closer to God. Those who understand this willingly submit themselves to the knowledge that God is in control. He is there in the lion's den. The soldier of Christ knows that God's army is oiled by the discipline of trials. He is training for battle, and in the light of that objective, the yoke of Jesus is therefore easy and the burden is light. He has not been *drafted* into the army of God, but he has *willingly submitted* himself to the yoke of Christ. He knows that whatever affliction, trial, or weight of resistance comes his way, comes only by the will of his God, that "all things work together for good to those who love God, to those who are called according to His purpose."[105] And His purpose is the reach the lost.

There goes another minute. *Gone forever.* Go share your faith while you still have time.

TICK ...
TICK ...
TICK ...
TICK ...
TICK ...
TICK ...
TICK ...
TICK ...
TICK ...
TICK ...
TICK ...
TICK ...
TICK ...
TICK ...
TICK ...
TICK ...
TICK ...
TICK ...
TICK ...
TICK ...
TICK ...
TICK ...
TICK ...
TICK ...
TICK ...
TICK ...
TICK ...
TICK ...
TICK ...

If I Had My Way

Bible teacher, Paris Reidhead, said, "If I had my way, I would declare a moratorium on public preaching of 'the plan of salvation' in America for one to two years. Then I would call on everyone who has use of the airwaves and the pulpits to preach the holiness of God, the righteousness of God, and the Law of God until sinners would cry out, 'What must we do to be saved?' Then I would take them off in a corner and whisper the Gospel to them. Don't use John 3:16. Such drastic action is needed because we have Gospel-hardened a generation of sinners by telling them how to be saved before they have any understanding why they need to be saved." What wise words from a man who understood the principles of biblical evangelism. May God give us the same wisdom.

There goes another minute.
Gone forever. Go share your faith
while you still have time.

The Father of us All

The Apostle Paul called Abraham, "the father of us all."[106] He had that title because he had great faith *in* and did great things *for* God. Abraham knew that He kept every promise He had made. We are told, "He staggered not at the promise of God through unbelief; but was strong in faith, giving glory to God; and being fully persuaded that, what he had promised, he was able also to perform."[107] Do we have that same faith? If you study the life of Abraham, you will see that he was obedient by leaving his home to do God's will. He was unselfish toward Lot. He was courageous, kind, and prayerful, and of course, he had great faith in God. He had all this without the great benefit of being born again. How much more then should we achieve great things for God?

There goes another minute.
Gone forever. Go share your faith
while you still have time.

TICK ...
TICK ...
TICK ...
TICK ...
TICK ...
TICK ...
TICK ...
TICK ...
TICK ...
TICK ...
TICK ...
TICK ...
TICK ...
TICK ...
TICK ...
TICK ...
TICK ...
TICK ...
TICK ...
TICK ...
TICK ...
TICK ...
TICK ...
TICK ...
TICK ...
TICK ...
TICK ...

The Tiniest Details

Do you ever think about the mind of God? He knows the tiniest details of every atom ten thousands miles down into the depth of the sun. He knows the thoughts of a flea hidden in the fur on the back of a wild Alaskan bear. He even knows your name, your thoughts, and how many hairs are on your head. No wonder the Psalmist says, "Great is the Lord and greatly to be praised; and His greatness is unsearchable."[108] Paul says, "Oh, the depth of the riches both of the wisdom and knowledge of God! How unsearchable are His judgments and His ways past finding out! For who has known the mind of the Lord?"[109] And yet, if you are a Christian, this same Almighty God, who dwells everywhere and knows all things, promises to be with you today.

There goes another minute.
Gone forever. Go share your faith
while you still have time.

The First Contact

Much of unregenerate contemporary humanity is bent on prejudice when it comes to the things of God. Their limited knowledge leaves them with a prejudicial attitude. They have been programmed into thinking that we are fanatical, religious "fundamentalists." However, if they only knew what we have in Christ, if they could only have the light of understanding about the issues of eternity, they would listen with bated breath. This is why our first contact with an unsaved person is so important. We can't let them justify their prejudice. While we speak to them on a natural level, they should be feeling the warmth of a genuine, sincere heart. Then, when they find that we are Christians, they should be saying within their minds, "This person is different." So, let the warmth of God's love be evident every time you make contact with any unsaved person.

There goes another minute.
Gone forever. **Go share your faith while you still have time.**

Burn the Carpet

Early in 1993, in Auckland, New Zealand, a small group of people moved into an old jewelry factory to conduct their church services. After cleaning the building, they were left with a pile of dust, which someone had the good sense to take to a gold refinery, *where it yielded $8,500 in gold dust!* When the refinery asked if they could burn the carpet, the church group gave them a piece, which was 12 feet square. It produced $3,500 worth of gold. They also vacuumed $350 worth of gold dust from the ceiling. We are nothing but dust that God has saved and separated. He knows that the heat of fiery trials will separate the dirt from things of great value. The fire produces in us that which is precious in His sight, so that we are then fit for the Master's use. And use us He will ... if we are willing.

There goes another minute.
Gone forever. Go share your faith
while you still have time.

The Debarked Dog

A man in California had his noisy dog debarked. One of the saddest sights you can see is a dog barking frantically with no noise coming out of its mouth. A man passing by saw this man standing at his gate with his dog, and approached the animal to pat it. Just as the dog opened its mouth to bark at the stranger, the animal's owner said, "No bark!" The dog opened its mouth and no noise came out. The stranger was *very* impressed with what he saw as incredible obedience. Some preachers are like that dog. They look like preachers and they go through the motions of preaching, but the *bark* of the Gospel is never heard coming from their mouths. They speak of faith, healing, the anointing, prayer, praise, the promises, prosperity, and power. They speak of everything *but* sin, righteousness, and judgment to come. Don't be like them.

**There goes another minute.
Gone forever. Go share your faith
while you still have time.**

Keep Your Fears to Yourself

Robert Louis Stevenson said, "Keep your fears to yourself, but share your courage with others." The children of Israel were told not to speak as they walked around the walls of Jericho. What they were doing was foolish. They were opening themselves to the ridicule of the enemy. It would have been hard to say anything positive, but when they did say something in the form of a unified shout, it brought the downfall of the enemy, not their brethren. One of Satan's biggest lies is to tell Christians that to witness for Christ is difficult. To say that we are unable to witness is to say that God's promise of help is empty. If I say, "I can't" when God's Word says, "I can do *all* things through Christ who strengthens me,"[110] I am choosing a lie rather than the truth. So, keep your fears to yourself, and share your courage with others.

There goes another minute.
Gone forever. **Go share your faith while you still have time.**

Free Fuel:
The Lighthouse Keeper

A lighthouse keeper regularly gave free fuel to ships that miscalculated fuel needed to reach the port to which they were heading. One night during a storm, lightning struck his lighthouse and put out his light. He immediately turned on his generator, but it soon ran out of fuel because he had given his reserves to passing ships. During the dark night, a ship struck rocks and many lives were lost. At his trial, the judge knew the lighthouse keeper was a kind man, and he wept as he gave sentence. He accused him of neglecting his primary responsibility — to keep the light shining. The Church can so often get caught up in legitimate acts of kindness — standing for political righteousness, etc., but our primary task is to keep the light of the Gospel shining so that sinners can avoid the jagged-edged rocks of wrath and escape being eternally damned.

There goes another minute.
Gone forever. Go share your faith
while you still have time.

Into a Far Country

The prodigal son went into a far country and spent his money on parties and prostitutes, but when a famine came on the land and his money ran out, the only work he could find was feeding pigs. As he watched the pigs eat, he wanted to pick up their filthy food and eat it himself, and it was that thought that brought him to his senses. Did you also try to get far away from God so that you could enjoy the pleasures of sin? Did you come to the realization that your desires were unclean? Did you then run to God and find that He was ready to meet you halfway? He gave you a robe of righteousness to cover your filth, an inheritance ring for your finger, and Gospel shoes for your feet. There are other lost prodigals out there. They are waiting for you to speak to them.

There goes another minute.
Gone forever. Go share your faith
while you still have time.

God is Our Friend

Probably the greatest deception blinding humanity is the sin of self-righteousness. They think that they are good enough to go to Heaven. This deception is there because they think that they already have peace with God — that He is their friend, and they are His delight. What we must do (with the help of God) is place them on the docket of God's Courtroom. They must see that they are guilty criminals in His sight, deeply in debt to His Law, and desperately in need of His mercy. This is why God's Law is not only "perfect, holy, just and good," but it is "wonderful." It shows the sinner that God isn't their friend, but their enemy, because they have greatly offended Him. Yet, there is mercy for those who will call upon the name of Jesus. Time is short. The door of mercy will soon close.

There goes another minute.
Gone forever. Go share your faith
while you still have time.

Cute Little Angels

The world sees angels as those cute little creatures with wings that they hang on their Christmas trees. Yet the Bible speaks of mighty angels before whom hardened Roman soldiers fainted like dead men. God used angels to stop Pharaoh and his army, to stop the mouths of Daniel's lions, to awaken Peter as he slept in prison, and to encourage the Apostle Paul when he was caught in a great storm. But the work of angels isn't finished. They can minister to us also. The Scriptures says, "But to which of the angels has He ever said: 'Sit at My right hand, Till I make Your enemies Your footstool'? Are they not all ministering spirits sent forth to minister for those who will inherit salvation?"[111] May God send His angels to help you today.

There goes another minute.
Gone forever. Go share your faith
while you still have time.

As Sly as a Fox

What words do you think of when you hear of these animals—the weasel, the fox, and the snake? Do you think of "sly," "sneaky," and "subtle?" What word enters your mind when you think a lamb? Perhaps the word "helpless" comes to mind? Jesus was called the "Lamb" of God. He came to this earth as a helpless, sacrificial lamb to die for sin of this evil world. As he stood as a lamb before Pilate, He offered no resistance. He gave His back to the smiters, and His beard to those who ripped it from His chin. He gave His head to the crown of thorns, His face to those who spat on Him, and His hands and feet to the soldiers who nailed them to the cross. He gave His life for us, so that we could have life forever. He *proved* His love for us. We must prove our love for Him.

There goes another minute.
Gone forever. Go share your faith
while you still have time.

The Sentence of Condemnation

Listen to Jonathan Edwards describe the state of the lost. In his famous sermon (*Sinners in the Hands of an Angry God*), he said, "They are already under a sentence of condemnation to Hell. They do not only justly deserve to be cast down [there], but the sentence of the Law of God, that eternal and immutable rule of righteousness that God has fixed between Him and mankind, is gone out against them, and stands against them; so that they are bound over already to Hell. John 3:18 [says] 'He that believeth not is condemned already.' So, that every unconverted man properly belongs to Hell; that is his place; from [there] he is, John 8:23: 'You are from beneath.' And there be is bound; it is the place that justice, and God's word, and the sentence of his unchangeable Law assign to him."

There goes another minute.
Gone forever. Go share your faith
while you still have time.

God's Tolerance

The world doesn't understand that God sees their thought-life. The Bible says, "The Lord does not see as man sees; for man looks at the outward appearance, but the Lord looks at the heart."[112] The world also makes the mistake of thinking that God's moral standards are the same as theirs. They presume that He tolerates lying and stealing, and that He isn't too concerned about murder and adultery. This is why we must use God's Law to bring the knowledge of sin and show it to be exceedingly sinful. We do that by opening it up to show its spiritual nature—that God requires truth in the inward parts—that He considers lust to be adultery, and hatred to be murder. That knowledge helps to drive sinners toward the mercy of God in Christ.

There goes another minute.
Gone forever. **Go share your faith while you still have time.**

The Salt of the Earth

Jesus said, "You are the salt of the earth; but if the salt loses its flavor, how shall it be seasoned? It is then good for nothing but to be thrown out and trampled under foot by men."[113] Salt cleanses; it preserves; it brings out taste. If you want to cleanse a stain from a cup, use salt. If you want to preserve meat from rotting, use salt. If you want to bring out the flavor of food, use salt. It has many properties, but the one common denominator is that it must come into contact with something to do its work. It needs to be scattered out of the saltshaker. If we don't shake ourselves into reaching the lost, God may shake us. Remember, He allowed Saul of Tarsus to scatter the early Church. We are told that they were "scattered abroad, and went everywhere preaching the word."[114]

There goes another minute.
Gone forever. Go share your faith
while you still have time.

The Image of God

The Second of the Ten Commandments says, "You shall not make yourself a graven image." When the world makes a god with their hands, they break that Commandment, but they also violate the Moral Law when they make an image of God in their minds. That's called "idolatry," and we are told that idolaters will not inherit the Kingdom of God. When we tell sinners what the Law requires, it shows them that they have fallen short of God's standard. The Law of God brings the knowledge of sin. It calls for our blood, and demands our death and damnation. When a sinful world understands that, they are ready for the Good News that Christ redeemed us from the curse of the Law, being made a curse for us. The Law makes the cross make sense. That's why Jesus used it. That's why Paul used it. Do the same.

There goes another minute.
Gone forever. **Go share your faith**
while you still have time.

Pointless Grace

It was John MacArthur who wrote, "Grace means nothing to a person who does not know he is sinful and that such sinfulness means he is separated from God and damned. It is therefore pointless to preach grace until the impossible demands of the Law and the reality of guilt before God are preached." This is as simple as telling a patient that he is sick *before* telling him that he needs a cure. Why would any patient want a cure if he isn't first convinced that he is sick? Those who fail to adhere to this biblical principle may impress with large numbers who profess faith in Jesus, but time will almost certainly prove them to be false converts. The Law must precede the Gospel to convince the sinner that he needs the Savior. Charles Spurgeon said, "I do not believe that any man can preach the Gospel who does not preach the Law."

There goes another minute.
Gone forever. **Go share your faith while you still have time.**

TICK ...

Serial Liars

Back in 1991, 20,000 middle- and high-school students were surveyed by the Josephson Institute of Ethics—a nonprofit organization in Marina del Rey, California, devoted to character education. Ninety-two percent of the teenagers admitted having lied to their parents in the previous year, and 73 percent characterized themselves as "serial liars," meaning they told lies weekly. Despite these admissions, 91 percent of all respondents said they were "satisfied with my own ethics and character."[115] They were satisfied with their own ethics because they were ignorant of God's ethics, and the standard by which He will judge them on Judgment Day. These kids are typical of today's generation, and they need to be confronted with God's Law to show them God's righteousness, and the terrible result of bearing false witness. The Bible warns, "All liars will have their part in the lake of fire."[116]

There goes another minute.
Gone forever. **Go share your faith while you still have time.**

TICK ...
TICK ...
TICK ...
TICK ...
TICK ...
TICK ...
TICK ...
TICK ...
TICK ...
TICK ...
TICK ...
TICK ...
TICK ...
TICK ...
TICK ...
TICK ...
TICK ...
TICK ...
TICK ...
TICK ...
TICK ...
TICK ...
TICK ...
TICK ...
TICK ...
TICK ...
TICK ...
TICK ...

Heaven Without Hell

It was the founder of the Salvation Army, William Booth, who warned, "The chief danger of the 20th Century will be religion without the Holy Spirit, Christianity without Christ, forgiveness without repentance, salvation without regeneration, politics without God, and heaven without Hell." His words were partially fulfilled in the 20th Century, but how true they have become nowadays. Heaven is preached without Hell. Forgiveness is offered without the necessity of repentance. We have forsaken the straight gate, and opened it wide for the lost, and now much of the Church looks and acts no different from the world. The only answer to this dilemma is to thunder the fear of God from the pulpit. It is through the fear of the Lord that men depart from sin, and they won't do that as long as we compromise our message.

**There goes another minute.
Gone forever. Go share your faith
while you still have time.**

Mere Lip Service

Listen to what Nobel prize-winning American physicist Steven Weinberg said in a recent PBS interview regarding religion: "I have very good friends who belong to religious denominations whose teaching is that since I don't accept their teaching, I am damned for all eternity. And you would think that these friends would try to convert me. *But they never do.* Now, you could explain this in various ways. It may be that they really don't like me very much and are just as glad to see me damned for all eternity—that's a possible explanation. But another explanation which I tend to think is more likely is that although they know what their church teaches, they give lip service to it." Our unconcern for the lost shows that we merely give God's threat of Hell mere lip service. Shame on us.

There goes another minute.
Gone forever. Go share your faith
while you still have time.

TICK ...

Lack of Knowledge

TICK ...
TICK ...
TICK ...
TICK ...
TICK ...
TICK ...
TICK ...
TICK ...
TICK ...
TICK ...
TICK ...
TICK ...
TICK ...
TICK ...
TICK ...
TICK ...
TICK ...

Hosea 4:6 is often quoted out of context. It says, "My people are destroyed for lack of knowledge." That's where the verse is often ended. But the Bible gives us details as to the lack of knowledge. We are told in the same verse " ... Because you have forgotten the law of your God, I also will forget your children." When the Law of God is rejected, it leaves us without the knowledge of sin. Paul said, "I had not known sin, but by the law."[117] And if there is no knowledge of sin, we understandably see no need to repent. And Jesus warned that unless we repent, we will perish.[118] So, make sure you do what Jesus did. When you are witnessing to someone, use the Law to bring the knowledge of sin, so that they will see their need of the Savior.[119]

TICK ...
TICK ...
TICK ...

**There goes another minute.
Gone forever. Go share your faith
while you still have time.**

TICK ...
TICK ...
TICK ...
TICK ...
TICK ...
TICK ...
TICK ...

God and Natural Disasters

The world is offended by the thought that God would send natural disasters. Their concept of Him is one of love and mercy. Yet, their God allows 40,000 children to die of starvation every 24 hours. He also lets thousands die in earthquakes and hurricanes. The truth is, the concept of God is a figment of their sinful imaginations. The true God warns, "Because you disdained all my counsel, and would have none of my rebuke, I also will laugh at your calamity; I will mock when your terror comes, when your terror comes like a storm, and your destruction comes like a whirlwind, when distress and anguish come upon you. Then they will call on me, but I will not answer; They will seek me diligently, but they will not find me."[120] It is wise for us to therefore fear God, and listen to His counsel.

There goes another minute.
Gone forever. Go share your faith
while you still have time.

TICK ...
TICK ...
TICK ...
TICK ...
TICK ...
TICK ...
TICK ...
TICK ...
TICK ...
TICK ...
TICK ...
TICK ...
TICK ...
TICK ...
TICK ...
TICK ...
TICK ...
TICK ...
TICK ...
TICK ...
TICK ...
TICK ...
TICK ...
TICK ...
TICK ...
TICK ...
TICK ...
TICK ...

265

Are Your Crazy?

When a politician once suggested that in the light of natural disasters, we should examine ourselves morally as a nation, his interviewer was infuriated. He couldn't believe for a moment that God had anything to do with disasters that take human life. He said, "When men came to Jesus in Luke 13, and asked about a tower that had fallen on eighteen men and killed them, asking if God had anything to do with it, Jesus answered 'Are you crazy!?!'" Not quite. He actually warned those who asked, "Unless you repent, you will all likewise perish." While none of us can say of a certainty *when* God sends judgment, when natural disasters take human life we should fear God and obey His command to repent and trust the Savior, or we will also perish. That's the message we should never fear to give.

There goes another minute.
Gone forever. Go share your faith
while you still have time.

Order of Service

As soldiers of Christ, we have been called into active service, but most of us have been more concerned about the *order of* service, than our *orders for* service. We have our battle orders from Headquarters of Heaven to seek out those who are enemies of God in their minds through wicked works. We are to persuade and compel them to desert their sin. They must defect before the Great Day of Battle, when the ultimate weapon of Eternal Justice will be unleashed against sinful mankind. On that Day, there will be no neutral ground ... they will suffer the vengeance of eternal fire. God's justice will be thorough. Our message is "Surrender or be damned. Become a citizen of the Kingdom of Heaven or forever be banished from its gates by the King of Kings into everlasting fire prepared for the devil and his angels."

There goes another minute.
Gone forever. Go share your faith
while you still have time.

TICK ...
TICK ...
TICK ...
TICK ...
TICK ...
TICK ...
TICK ...
TICK ...
TICK ...
TICK ...
TICK ...
TICK ...
TICK ...
TICK ...
TICK ...
TICK ...
TICK ...
TICK ...
TICK ...
TICK ...
TICK ...
TICK ...
TICK ...
TICK ...
TICK ...
TICK ...
TICK ...
TICK ...

Admonitions to War

The Bible is unashamedly filled with admonitions to war.[121] We are told to fight the good fight of faith. We have been sent as emissaries of peace to diplomatically plead with the ungodly to lay down their weapons. But in a world that hates its Creator, we are forced to precede the offer of peace with the threat of war. We must therefore mobilize as a mighty, militant, aggressive army, spearheading attacks through the power of prayer. We must ransack the barracks of Hell and penetrate the territories of the devil with the flag of righteousness and the trumpet of victory resounding. "Retreat" is not an option. If we fall back in battle, it is merely to muster forces and regain our spirit. We know that our strengths are the enemy's weaknesses. He crumbles before the powers of holiness, righteousness, justice, virtue, morality, and truth.

**There goes another minute.
Gone forever. Go share your faith
while you still have time.**

Casual in Prayer

As soldiers of Christ, we are told to fight the good fight of faith. Our prayer life energizes our evangelism. We know that we mustn't be casual in prayer, or we will be casualties in war. We give no place to the devil or he will take the place we give him and work toward our defeat. But that is not an option, because it is God who teaches our hands to war. The weapons of our warfare are not carnal, but mighty through God to the pulling down of strongholds. The very finger of God has issued to us the Ten Great Cannons of His Law. The ground troops lie low in humility while the cannons blast over their heads of our enemies into their souls. There is no greater artillery in our arsenal to break the spirit of the adversary, to weaken his lines of defense, or to send terror into his heart.

There goes another minute.
Gone forever. Go share your faith
while you still have time.

The Good Fight of Faith

We are in the middle of a heated battle for the souls of the lost. "No fear!" is our battle cry, and boldness, our battering ram. We will have no draft dodgers, no cowards, no AWOL, no withdrawal, no cease-fire, and *no* surrender! If God is for us, *nothing* can be against us. We are more than conquerors through Him that loved us, and though a host shall encamp against us, we shall not be afraid. Silence is the enemy that we will not let into our ranks. The walls of Jericho have been encompassed. We have been silent for too long—it is time to shout down the strongholds of the enemy. By the Grace of our God, we will triumph over evil, for that is the struggle for which we contest. We fight the *good* fight of faith, so muster your courage, lift up hands that hang down and strengthen feeble knees.

There goes another minute. *Gone forever.* Go share your faith while you still have time.

TICK ...
TICK ...
TICK ...
TICK ...
TICK ...
TICK ...
TICK ...
TICK ...
TICK ...
TICK ...
TICK ...
TICK ...
TICK ...
TICK ...
TICK ...
TICK ...
TICK ...
TICK ...
TICK ...
TICK ...
TICK ...
TICK ...
TICK ...
TICK ...
TICK ...
TICK ...
TICK ...
TICK ...

Don't Break Ranks

Never let the enemy have you believe you are alone in your battle to reach the lost. Throughout the world is a loyal infantry made up of men and women who are strategically placed by God. They are unseen through the fog of distance, but they are unified in purpose. Veteran soldiers who have died before us symbolically surround us as a crowd of witnesses to applaud our every advance. Don't break ranks. Strive for the unity of the Gospel, following the Captain of the Lord of Hosts who is leading the charge. Through our God, we shall do valiantly, for it is He who shall tread down our enemies. Let the trumpet make a certain sound! Hear its soul-stirring sound, and let the stirred soul lift up the flaming sword! The high praises of God are in our mouths. The two-edged Sword of God's Word is in our hands.

**There goes another minute.
Gone forever. Go share your faith
while you still have time.**

TICK ... TICK ...

Our Battle Cry

As soldiers of Christ, our battle cry is "Give me liberty to preach, or give me death!" We only enlist those who will fling caution to the wind, and who will join an invasion of tooth-gritting, uncompromising, unyielding, relentless evangelism. We must assault the enemy with spiritual snipers, godly guerrillas, soul-loving storm troopers, counter-attacking on the right hand and on the left. Our weapons are love, faith, goodness, mercy, and gentleness. If the world spurns us, if our blood is spilled on the soil of this sinful world for the cause of the Gospel, so be it. If our Commander catches our tears in a bottle, how much more will He value our blood poured out on the earth? The foundation of the Church was laid in the soil of a bloody hill, and soaked with the blood of Stephen and a multitude who "waxed valiant in fight."

There goes another minute.
Gone forever. Go share your faith
while you still have time.

The Supreme Sacrifice

If, as soldiers of the cross, we have also been crucified with Christ, it is no great thing to give the supreme sacrifice. We crave armed forces who will lunge at the devil, who will let him feel the heat of the sharp two-edged sword, and who will free those who are "taken captive to do his will." We want chivalrous, undaunted, valiant, noble warriors—loyalists, patriots, advocates of righteousness, defenders of the faith, upholders of the truth within our garrisons to force back Satan and his hellish hordes. We must have soul-thirsty soldiers, self-sacrificial "kamikaze" Christians. We ache for 21st Century soldiers who are not afraid to bear the marks of the Lord Jesus. May God give us those who will give themselves in the final battle for the souls of men and women, without reserve, to radical, revolutionary, God-pleasing, militant evangelism.

**There goes another minute.
Gone forever. Go share your faith
while you still have time.**

Under Running Water

Did you know that the Bible contains many medical and scientifically accurate facts, and these were written thousands of years before modern science discovered them? For example, 3,000 years ago, when the scientists believed that the earth was a flat disk, the Book of Isaiah was scientifically accurate when it spoke of the earth as being a sphere. The Book of Job was scientifically accurate when it said that the earth had a free float in space. At the time, scientists believed that the earth sat on a large animal. Over 1,000 years before Christ, when dealing with disease, the Book of Leviticus *insisted* that hands should be washed under *running* water.[122] For thousands of years doctors washed their hands in standing water. If they had believed the Bible and had done what it said to do, multitudes wouldn't have died because of their unhygienic practices.

There goes another minute.
Gone forever. Go share your faith
while you still have time.

TICK ...
TICK ...
TICK ...
TICK ...
TICK ...
TICK ...
TICK ...
TICK ...
TICK ...
TICK ...
TICK ...
TICK ...
TICK ...
TICK ...
TICK ...
TICK ...
TICK ...
TICK ...
TICK ...
TICK ...
TICK ...
TICK ...
TICK ...
TICK ...
TICK ...
TICK ...

Signs of the Times

The Scriptures predict that in the days preceding the "end of this age" there will be earthquakes in different parts of the world, increased violence, nation rising against nation, wars, and a breakdown of marriage. There will be famines, disease, a 'form of godliness,' money-hungry preachers deceiving multitudes and slurring the name of Christianity, a denial of a worldwide flood, skeptics saying that these 'signs' have always been around, and the Jews possessing Jerusalem. The Jews obtained Jerusalem in 1967 after being without a homeland for 2,000 years, bringing into culmination all these signs of the times. The Bible also predicted that in these days, Jerusalem would become a burden to all nations. The Bible is God's revelation of Himself and His purposes. It has the fingerprints of divine inspiration all over it.

There goes another minute.
Gone forever. **Go share your faith while you still have time.**

TICK ...
TICK ...
TICK ...
TICK ...
TICK ...
TICK ...
TICK ...
TICK ...
TICK ...
TICK ...
TICK ...
TICK ...
TICK ...
TICK ...
TICK ...
TICK ...
TICK ...
TICK ...
TICK ...
TICK ...
TICK ...
TICK ...
TICK ...
TICK ...
TICK ...
TICK ...
TICK ...
TICK ...

Words Without Precedent

We often take the words of Jesus for granted. Take for instance His "Heaven and earth will pass away, but My words will by no means pass away."[123] He said that just after He listed what we commonly call "the signs of the times." He spoke about things that would come to pass 2,000 years after the time in which He said them. He, with 100 percent accuracy, predicted the future. Modern science struggles to accurately predict tomorrow's weather. He also said that heaven and earth would pass away before His words passed away. Try saying something profound today and see if people remember it tomorrow, let alone 2,000 years latter. The words of Jesus are without precedent, without comparison, without the scope of human foundation … because Jesus was no ordinary Man. He was God in human form, our Lord, Savior, and coming King.

There goes another minute.
Gone forever. Go share your faith
while you still have time.

The Inspiration of Scripture

The Bible doesn't attempt to defend its inspiration. Genesis simply opens with the words, "God said." The phrase, "The Lord spoke," is used 560 times in the first five books of the Bible and at least 3,800 times in the whole of the Old Testament. Isaiah claims at least 40 times that his message came directly from God; Ezekiel, 60 times; and Jeremiah, 100 times. There are about 3,856 verses directly or indirectly concerned with prophecy in Scripture. Mormons, Buddhists, and Muslims have what they consider their own sacred writings, but the element of *proven* prophecy is absent from them. The same is true of any other books in any of the world's religions. Most people are not aware that the Bible was written over a period of 1,600 years by more than 40 authors on hundreds of controversial subjects, and yet they penned their words in absolute harmony.

**There goes another minute.
Gone forever. Go share your faith
while you still have time.**

TICK ...
TICK ...
TICK ...
TICK ...
TICK ...
TICK ...
TICK ...
TICK ...
TICK ...
TICK ...
TICK ...
TICK ...
TICK ...
TICK ...
TICK ...
TICK ...
TICK ...
TICK ...
TICK ...
TICK ...
TICK ...
TICK ...
TICK ...
TICK ...
TICK ...

Praying for Revival

C. T. Studd said, "We Christians too often substitute prayer for playing the game. Prayer is good; but when used as a substitute for obedience, it is nothing but a blatant hypocrisy, a despicable Pharisaism . . . to your knees, man! And to your Bible! Decide at once! Don't hedge! Time flies! Cease your insults to God. Quit consulting flesh and blood. Stop your lame, lying, and cowardly excuses." A. W. Tozer said a similar thing: "Have you noticed how much praying for revival has been going on of late—and how little revival has resulted? I believe the problem is that we have been trying to substitute praying for obeying, and it simply will not work. To pray for revival while ignoring the plain precept laid down in Scripture is to waste a lot of words and get nothing for our trouble. Prayer will become effective when we stop using it as a substitute for obedience."

There goes another minute.
Gone forever. Go share your faith
while you still have time.

Kill the Fleas

Paul reminded Timothy to stir up the gift that God had given him. Then the Apostle addressed "the spirit of fear."[124] If you evangelize, you will be familiar with the spirit of fear. It hangs around the evangelistic Christian as fleas hang around a dog. Fear will be on your back the moment you decide to do something to reach the lost. It will try to get its sharp teeth into your flesh and inject its irritating poison. But Paul gave Timothy a repellant. He said that he had received the Spirit of "power, love, and a sound mind."[125] Jesus told His disciples to wait on God for that "power."[126] The promised power overcomes our fears. It kills the fleas. Paul then exhorts Timothy to be unashamed of the Gospel. So kill the fleas and let love have its way.

There goes another minute.
Gone forever. Go share your faith
while you still have time.

You Missed the Resurrection!

The Bible exhorts us, "But shun profane and vain babblings: for they will increase unto more ungodliness. And their word will eat as does a canker: of whom is Hymenaeus and Philetus; Who concerning the truth have erred, saying that the resurrection is past already; and overthrow the faith of some."[127] Hymenaeus and Philetus preached that the resurrection had passed. So, some folks "backslid." Their faith was "overthrown." Think about it. These two preached, "The resurrection has passed. You missed out!" So, some who professed faith in Jesus had their faith overthrown. They believed what these men said over what the Word of God said. In essence, they said, "God is a liar. His promises aren't to be trusted. I'm going back to the world." But true converts don't fall away. They trust the promise, which says, "*Whosoever* calls upon the name of the Lord *shall* be saved."[128]

There goes another minute. *Gone forever.* Go share your faith while you still have time.

Terrible Trials

Are you going through terrible trials? Don't let them steal your joy. It's normal for a Christian to have trial after trial. Listen to Scripture: "In this you greatly rejoice, though now for a little while, if need be, you have been grieved by various trials, that the genuineness of your faith, being much more precious than gold that perishes, though it is tested by fire, may be found to praise, honor, and glory at the revelation of Jesus Christ, whom having not seen you love."[129] The great key to trials is to keep seeking the lost *while* you are in the fire. Don't let your time be wasted. When you are a soldier under fire, that's when you should be fighting the hardest. The enemy wants you to lay down your weapons and surrender. Don't think of it for a moment.

There goes another minute.
Gone forever. **Go share your faith while you still have time.**

TICK ...
TICK ...
TICK ...
TICK ...
TICK ...
TICK ...
TICK ...
TICK ...
TICK ...
TICK ...
TICK ...
TICK ...
TICK ...
TICK ...
TICK ...
TICK ...
TICK ...
TICK ...
TICK ...
TICK ...
TICK ...
TICK ...
TICK ...
TICK ...
TICK ...
TICK ...
TICK ...

The Most Precious Substance

What is the most precious substance on earth? Is it the gold? Is it human life? No. There was only one thing that God saw that was precious enough to buy our redemption. It was the precious blood of Christ. Listen to the Bible: "... conduct yourselves throughout the time of your sojourning here in fear; knowing that you were not redeemed with corruptible things, like silver or gold, from your aimless conduct received by tradition from your fathers, but with the precious blood of Christ, as of a lamb without blemish and without spot."[130] On that dark night in Egypt when death fell upon the land, it was the blood of a spotless lamb that secured the lives of the Hebrews. How much more shall the precious blood of the Lamb of God redeem the lost?

There goes another minute. *Gone forever*. Go share your faith while you still have time.

Stirring the Troops

Perhaps you need some encouragement today. Listen to Moses (at the age of 120 years) stir his troops: "Be strong and of good courage, do not fear nor be afraid of them; for the Lord your God, He is the One who goes with you. He will not leave you nor forsake you."[131] Now listen to King David stir his own soul: "I will not be afraid of ten thousands of people who have set themselves against me all around."[132] And Isaiah the prophet: "Behold, God is my salvation; I will trust, and not be afraid: for the Lord Jehovah is my strength and my song; he also is become my salvation. Therefore with joy shall you draw water out of the wells of salvation."[133] The living waters have been drawn from the well of Calvary's cross. Take courage, and take them with joy to this dying world.

There goes another minute.
Gone forever. **Go share your faith while you still have time.**

TICK ...
TICK ...
TICK ...
TICK ...
TICK ...
TICK ...
TICK ...
TICK ...
TICK ...
TICK ...
TICK ...
TICK ...
TICK ...
TICK ...
TICK ...
TICK ...
TICK ...
TICK ...
TICK ...
TICK ...
TICK ...
TICK ...
TICK ...
TICK ...
TICK ...
TICK ...
TICK ...
TICK ...
TICK ...
TICK ...
TICK ...
TICK ...
TICK ...

Do It Yourself

There are some things in life that you have to do yourself. This was the case with the giving of the Law. God considered the Ten Commandments to be so important, He didn't trust anyone else to write them. He came down to earth and inscribed the Law Himself with His finger. When the Law demanded death for the woman caught in the act of adultery, He once again wrote with His finger. Perhaps this time He wrote the Ten Commandments, but this time it was in sand rather than in stone, showing us that because of the cross, sin could now be washed away by the sea of God's forgetfulness. The cross of Calvary made room for the mercy of God for the whole human race, and that mercy is still available today.

**There goes another minute.
Gone forever. Go share your faith
while you still have time.**

The Cause of Sexual Sin

Look at the context of this verse: "Therefore let him who thinks he stands take heed lest he fall. No temptation has overtaken you except such as is common to man; but God is faithful, who will not allow you to be tempted beyond what you are able, but with the temptation will also make the way of escape, that you may be able to bear it. Therefore, my beloved, flee from idolatry."[134] The preceding Scriptures were talking about Israel's sexual sin, and how it caused them to fall. Then we are told to look for a way of escape when we are tempted, and to flee "idolatry." Idolatry is the root cause of sexual sin. We can only get into willful sin when we get out of the fear of the Lord. If we fear God, we won't fanaticize with the mind, lust with the eye, or even consider temptation.

There goes another minute.
Gone forever. Go share your faith
while you still have time.

TICK ...
TICK ...
TICK ...
TICK ...
TICK ...
TICK ...
TICK ...
TICK ...
TICK ...
TICK ...
TICK ...
TICK ...
TICK ...
TICK ...
TICK ...
TICK ...
TICK ...
TICK ...
TICK ...
TICK ...
TICK ...
TICK ...
TICK ...
TICK ...
TICK ...
TICK ...

Praying With Open Eyes

Do you ever pray with your eyes open?
It seems that David did. The Psalms tell
us, "My voice You shall hear in the
morning, O Lord; In the morning I will
direct it to You, And I will look up."[135]
Jesus prayed with His eyes open when
He stood outside the grave of Lazarus.
The Bible says, "And Jesus lifted up His
eyes and said, 'Father, I thank You that
You have heard Me.'"[136] Having our eyes
open now and then when we pray might
feel a little strange, but it helps us to
understand the omnipresence of
Almighty God. It reminds us that He
dwells everywhere. But notice where
David and Jesus looked. It was to the
heavens. When we pray looking up at the
heavens, it helps us not only to remember
that God is everywhere, but that He's
majestic, holy ... and almighty.

There goes another minute.
Gone forever. Go share your faith
while you still have time.

Growing Up Spiritually

One of the most exciting things about being a parent is seeing your child stand on his own two feet, feed himself, and show a concern for others. No parent wants to have a crawling, dependent, and selfish child. Have you grown to where you are standing on your own feet spiritually, or are you looking to others to hold you up? Are you feeding yourself daily on God's Word? Have you come to a point where you are concerned for others? If you have, you will reproduce of your own kind. If you seek and save the lost, you (with the help of God) will bring them through the door of genuine conversion. That means that they will be genuine converts who will also stand on their own two feet, feed themselves, and care about the salvation of the lost.

There goes another minute.
Gone forever. **Go share your faith while you still have time.**

TICK...
TICK...
TICK...
TICK...
TICK...
TICK...
TICK...
TICK...
TICK...
TICK...
TICK...
TICK...
TICK...
TICK...
TICK...
TICK...
TICK...
TICK...
TICK...
TICK...
TICK...
TICK...
TICK...
TICK...
TICK...
TICK...
TICK...

Fire in the Bones

Do you have a sense of overwhelming urgency when it comes to reaching the lost? Jeremiah did. He cried, "'I will not make mention of Him, nor speak anymore in His name.' But His word was in my heart like a burning fire shut up in my bones; I was weary of holding it back, and I could not."[137] The prophet Amos did. He said: "A lion has roared! Who will not fear? The Lord God has spoken! Who can but prophesy?"[138] Jesus did. He said, "I must work the works of Him who sent Me while it is day; the night is coming when no one can work."[139] So did the Apostle Paul: "For if I preach the Gospel, I have nothing to boast of, for necessity is laid upon me; yes, woe is me if I do not preach the Gospel!"[140] Don't hold back any longer.

There goes another minute. *Gone forever*. Go share your faith while you still have time.

They Are Ready

When David stood before Goliath, he said, "You come to me with a sword, with a spear, and with a javelin. But I come to you in the name of the Lord of hosts …" When we take the Gospel to this world, like Goliath, they are ready for battle. They are contentious, and refuse to obey the truth, but we come to them in the name of the Lord of hosts. We come to them in the name of Him who causes demons to tremble. It is through the name of Jesus that we access all the power of Heaven. The Bible says that if God is for us, nothing can be against us, and that the weapons we have in Christ are mighty through God to the pulling down of strongholds. So, never let fear hold you back. Instead, let faith push you forward.

**There goes another minute.
Gone forever. Go share your faith
while you still have time.**

TICK ...
TICK ...
TICK ...
TICK ...
TICK ...
TICK ...
TICK ...
TICK ...
TICK ...
TICK ...
TICK ...
TICK ...
TICK ...
TICK ...
TICK ...
TICK ...
TICK ...
TICK ...
TICK ...
TICK ...
TICK ...
TICK ...
TICK ...
TICK ...
TICK ...
TICK ...
TICK ...
TICK ...

289

Distasteful Sentiments

A great preacher once said, "I would rather hear it said, 'That man said something in his message that made many of the people think less of him; he uttered most distasteful sentiments; he did nothing but drive at us with the Word of the Lord while he was preaching. His one aim was to bring us to repentance and faith in Christ.' That is the kind of man whom the Lord delights to bless." He also said, "Ministers who do not aim to cut deep are not worth their salt. God never sent a man who never troubles men's consciences." How do you trouble the deadened consciences of a dying world? You preach the Moral Law coupled with the surety of future punishment. You speak of God's holiness and of His wrath. These are not things that the world wants to hear, but hear them they must if we want them to be saved.

**There goes another minute.
Gone forever. Go share your faith
while you still have time.**

Death Swallowed

In the Old Testament, God promised, "I will ransom them from the power of the grave; I will redeem them from death: O death, I will be your plagues …"[141] We had to be "ransomed" from the grave. We were held captive by the Law of sin and death in the same way a murderer is held captive by civil law. Isaiah also made promise of our rescue. He said, "He will swallow up death in victory."[142] This happened at the cross—"Jesus Christ … has abolished death and brought life and immortality to light through the Gospel."[143] Now God waits for us to fulfill His will so that the time will come when "God will wipe away every tear from their eyes; there shall be no more death, nor sorrow, nor crying; and there shall be no more pain …"[144]

There goes another minute.
Gone forever. Go share your faith
while you still have time.

Go About Doing Good

The Bible says of Jesus, "... God anointed Jesus of Nazareth with the Holy Spirit and with power, who went about doing good and healing all who were oppressed by the devil, for God was with Him."[145] If you are a Christian, God has also anointed you with the Holy Spirit. You too are to go about doing good. Be rich in good works. Show love and kindness wherever you can for the sake of the Gospel. You too can pray for those who are oppressed by the devil, because God is with you. No longer is He your enemy, but He's now your friend because of the cross. With all this going for you, make sure you don't waste your life on the futile and fleeting pleasures of this world. They are transient and superficial. Live for God and for His will and good pleasure.

**There goes another minute.
Gone forever. Go share your faith
while you still have time.**

That the Nations May Tremble

Don't you wish that God would release some of His power? Don't you wish that we had more of the supernatural in modern Christianity? Look at what happened in the Book of Acts after the disciples prayed: "And when they had prayed, the place where they were assembled together was shaken; and they were all filled with the Holy Spirit, and they spoke the word of God with boldness."[146] May our prayers cause an earthquake in the modern Church so that we would all be filled with the Holy Spirit and speak the Word with boldness. The prophet cried, "Oh, that You would rend the heavens! That You would come down! That the mountains might shake at Your presence ... to make Your name known to Your adversaries, that the nations may tremble at Your presence!"[147] May that be our earnest prayer.

There goes another minute.
Gone forever. Go share your faith
while you still have time.

A New Employer

Charlotte Gilman once said, "Death? Why this fuss about death? Use your imagination; try to visualize a world without death! … Death is the essential condition of life, not an evil." Her words sound brave, but they don't make sense. A world without death would be wonderful. Imagine a world where you never grow old and die. Nor do you lose those you love. While some in the world may have their thoughts about why death awaits each of us, the Bible tells us that it comes to us because it's a payment for wages that we have earned. It's exactly what each of us deserves, and we are told that we are held captive to the fear of death until we come to the Savior. But since the resurrection, we can have another Employer—Him who abolished death and brought life and immortality to light through the Gospel.

There goes another minute.
Gone forever. **Go share your faith while you still have time.**

TICK ...
TICK ...
TICK ...
TICK ...
TICK ...
TICK ...
TICK ...
TICK ...
TICK ...
TICK ...
TICK ...
TICK ...
TICK ...
TICK ...
TICK ...
TICK ...
TICK ...
TICK ...
TICK ...
TICK ...
TICK ...
TICK ...
TICK ...
TICK ...
TICK ...
TICK ...

A Fishing Hole

Do you have a fishing hole—a place where you deliberately go to mingle with the unsaved? You will more than likely need one, or you will go day after day without even speaking to an unsaved person, let alone witnessing to one. Even if you are in a large workplace, the time will come where you are fished out, and you will need to go to a fresh fishing hole, perhaps during your lunch hour. Ask God to direct you. It may be an area in your local mall where people sit. Or you may have to enroll in a gym or join a sports club so that you rub shoulders with the world. The Bible says that we should be "*in the midst* of a crooked and perverse nation, *among whom* we shine as lights *in the world*."[148] So, go beyond the walls of the monastery, and break your vow of silence.

**There goes another minute.
Gone forever. Go share your faith
while you still have time.**

TICK ...
TICK ...
TICK ...
TICK ...
TICK ...
TICK ...
TICK ...
TICK ...
TICK ...
TICK ...
TICK ...
TICK ...
TICK ...
TICK ...
TICK ...
TICK ...
TICK ...
TICK ...
TICK ...
TICK ...
TICK ...
TICK ...
TICK ...
TICK ...

295

Despise the Shame

When things get tough, we are to look "to Jesus the author and finisher of our faith; who for the joy that was set before him endured the cross, despising the shame, and is set down at the right hand of the throne of God."[149] We are to go to the cross and then to the throne. When our families look down on us religious fanatics, or people show condescension toward us because we gave them Gospel tracts, we are to *despise* the shame. The Greek word means, "to look down upon" it. We are to get above the shame, to make a miniature molehill out of what seems at that moment to be a mountain. What we go through for Christ is nothing compared to what He went through for us, and because He's on the throne, it's not worthy to be compared to the glory that shall be ours.[150]

There goes another minute. *Gone forever*. Go share your faith while you still have time.

Petrified Wood

Have you ever had a nightmare that was so terrifying that even when you woke up, you still felt overwhelmed with fear? At that point of time, you were "petrified." When wood is "petrified," it turns to stone. That's what fear can do to us. It can make us like stone. We become scared *stiff* to a point where we do nothing but sit like a rock on a pew. Yet, the love of God can take our stony hearts and make them tender. The Bible says that perfect love "casts out" fear.[151] So, when the enemy terrorizes you, think of the love of God in Christ. Think of the cross. Think of a fear that came to Jesus in the Garden of Gethsemane, and how His love for the Father enabled Him to cast out all fear, and drive Him to the cross. Think what Jesus did; then imitate Him.

There goes another minute.
Gone forever. Go share your faith
while you still have time.

TICK ...
TICK ...
TICK ...
TICK ...
TICK ...
TICK ...
TICK ...
TICK ...
TICK ...
TICK ...
TICK ...
TICK ...
TICK ...
TICK ...
TICK ...
TICK ...
TICK ...
TICK ...
TICK ...
TICK ...
TICK ...
TICK ...
TICK ...
TICK ...
TICK ...
TICK ...
TICK ...
TICK ...

297

Offended by Religion

Have you ever tried to talk to someone about the things of God, and the person has responded by saying that they weren't at all interested? If that happens, don't see it as a closed door. Try to look beyond their words to what they are communicating. Try to discern whether or not the person is offended by you personally or by what they may have perceived as "religious hypocrisy." It may be that some well-chosen words on your part at this point will open the door to a good conversation about the claims of the Gospel. Perhaps you could say, "Is it 'religion' that offends you? It offends me, too. There is so much hypocrisy." Or maybe you could gently say, "This is such an important issue. Couldn't you just give me two minutes? Please." Then pray that God opens the door.

There goes another minute.
Gone forever. Go share your faith
while you still have time.

Do You Buy Gifts?

How would you rate yourself on a "friendly" scale? How would other people rate you? Would you be a five, a seven, a ten? Aim to be a ten. Shoot for the clouds, and if you clear the trees, you're doing fine. Aim to be so friendly that people will enjoy your company and will want to interact with you in everyday conversation. Don't say, "But that's not my personality." If you are a Christian, you have the mind of Christ. You have the love of God dwelling in you, so let it out. Do you say kind things to people? Do you genuinely compliment them? Do you do buy gifts for them? Everyone loves a person who gives gifts. Do it for the sake of the Gospel. Do it to make people like you so that they will listen to you.

There goes another minute.
Gone forever. Go share your faith
while you still have time.

Fame and Fortune

Imagine you had a singing voice with that "something special." Your voice rocketed you to the top of pop charts worldwide. Even as a youth, you became a household name. You had fame and fortune. Everywhere you went, people gave you the best of things. Your money meant that you could do almost anything you wanted to in life ... almost anything. You couldn't see, because you were born blind. You had never seen a sunrise, a flower, color, or light. You had never even seen a human face. Would you swap your fame for sight? Who in his right mind wouldn't? Have you thanked God for your sight today? Are you grateful for not being born blind? Then prove your gratitude. Reach out to those who cannot see, and tell them that they need to be born again, so that they can see.

**There goes another minute.
Gone forever. Go share your faith
while you still have time.**

TICK ...

The Man in the Rowboat

A man in a rowboat once found himself caught in fast-moving water, heading for massive waterfall with jagged rocks 150 feet below. A passerby saw him rowing against the current, but his efforts were futile. Minute by minute the man in the rowboat was drawn closer and closer to the roaring falls. The passerby ran to his car, grabbed a rope from the trunk, and threw it to the boat. When it fell across the bow, he screamed, "Grab the rope! I'll pull you to the shore!" He couldn't believe his eyes. The man took no notice. He just kept rowing frantically against the current until he was sucked over the falls to his death. Therein lies the difference between being a Christian and being religious. For someone to be saved, he must cease his own religious labors, and trust alone in Jesus.

TICK ...
TICK ...
TICK ...
TICK ...
TICK ...
TICK ...
TICK ...
TICK ...
TICK ...
TICK ...
TICK ...
TICK ...
TICK ...
TICK ...
TICK ...
TICK ...
TICK ...
TICK ...
TICK ...
TICK ...
TICK ...

The Intellectual Issue

A well-known Christian apologist said that an evolutionary teacher told him that he thought that his case for creationism made scientific sense, but he said that he was going to continue to teach evolution. He said that as long as he believed that he was an animal, he could continue to live his life with no fear that he was morally responsible. He could do what he liked, and he could sleep with whom he wanted. The Christian apologist said that after speaking in seventy-nine countries on the subject of evolution, he was now convinced that evolution was not an intellectual issue. He said, "It is a *moral* issue." Why then do so many Christians try and deal with evolution as an intellectual issue? They should instead do what Jesus did. They should *make* it a moral issue by using God's Law to bring the knowledge of sin.

There goes another minute.
Gone forever. Go share your faith
while you still have time.

TICK ...
TICK ...
TICK ...
TICK ...
TICK ...
TICK ...
TICK ...

Lift Up Your Voice

Have you learned to probe the sinner's conscience? This is something each of us must learn to do if we want to see sinners come to genuine repentance, whether in one-to-one witnessing or in preaching. The conscience is waiting to be resurrected. It lies dormant in the dark human heart, waiting for you to speak to it. It is like an echo. It will remain silent as long as you remain silent. So do what the Bible tells you to do: "Cry aloud, spare not, lift up thy voice like a trumpet, and show my people their transgression, and the house of Jacob their sins."[152] When you trumpet the Law of Moses, if you listen carefully, you might hear the echo as the conscience "bears witness."[153] The conscience agrees with the Commandments. So, make sure you aim at the conscience when you speak to the lost. There goes another minute. Gone *forever*. Go share your faith while you still have time.

There goes another minute.
Gone forever. **Go share your faith**
while you still have time.

The Offer of Amnesty

Imagine that the police decided to offer amnesty for all lawbreakers. All charges would be dropped against those who had broken the law if, within a certain period of time, they surrendered their weapons. After the offer, there would be a massive bust in which every criminal would be rounded up and charged with his or her crimes. How do they present the good news of the amnesty? They make the police station attractive by chrome-plating the bars and carpeting the cells. Notices are then posted outside the station saying, "Come and hear the good news." Of course, the police would never think that anyone is going to visit a police station when they are guilty of breaking the law. Yet, this is the mentality of much of modern evangelism. The principle of *biblical* evangelism isn't to try to attract the world to us. It's to go to them.

There goes another minute.
Gone forever. Go share your faith
while you still have time.

304

Future Punishment

If the police offer an amnesty for criminals, they would probably run an advertisement saying something like: "The penalty for possessing any of the following weapons is a five-year imprisonment. If you surrender your weapon within seven days, we will not press charges. Remember, five long years—don't be foolish, take advantage of this amnesty now!" They wouldn't hesitate to speak of future punishment to lawbreakers. They would do this because the use of "fear" gets results. They are not alone. Fear is often used in advertising. In the late '90s the following was used in billboard advertising: "Diabetes—amputation, blindness, death. It's *that* serious." That is a scare tactic. It's using fear, but is legitimate, because they are stating the truth. So make sure you don't pull any punches. Speak the truth in love today.

There goes another minute.
Gone forever. **Go share your faith while you still have time.**

TICK ...
TICK ...
TICK ...
TICK ...
TICK ...
TICK ...
TICK ...
TICK ...
TICK ...
TICK ...
TICK ...
TICK ...
TICK ...
TICK ...
TICK ...
TICK ...
TICK ...
TICK ...
TICK ...
TICK ...
TICK ...
TICK ...
TICK ...
TICK ...
TICK ...
TICK ...

305

Avoiding Rabbit Trails

Stay aware of the enemy's tactic of sidetracking with "rabbit trails." Occasionally sinners have a genuine difficulty with "Darwin's theory," "hypocrites in the Church," etc., but in most cases they are nothing but "hedges." Sinners tend to make hedges, behind which they try to hide from God, as did Adam. The best way to get a sinner out from behind a hedge is to beat it with the rod of the Law, so that he stands exposed before his Creator. Get him to admit that he has lied, stolen, and looked with lust. If he says, "I don't believe in Judgment Day," just gently say, "That doesn't matter, you will still have to face God on Judgment Day, and you've admitted that you are a lying, thieving, adulterer at heart. God gave you a conscience so that you would know right from wrong. You will be without excuse."

There goes another minute.
Gone forever. Go share your faith
while you still have time.

The Voice of the Spirit

It's often asked if we should witness only to those to whom the Holy Spirit leads us to witness. We should *always* be sensitive God's leading, but we sometimes look for excuses to get out of the irksome task of evangelism, and frankly, not hearing the voice of the Spirit can easily become an excuse for us to walk past sinners without any concern for their salvation. So here's a good rule of thumb to help when it comes to sharing the Gospel: "Go in to all the world, and preach the Gospel to *every* creature."[154] Jesus said to witness to "*every* creature." Paul said, "For though I am free from all men, I have made myself a servant to all, that I might win the more,"[155] The Gospel is for *every* creature. It is for *all* people.

**There goes another minute.
Gone forever. Go share your faith
while you still have time.**

Did Not Know How to Answer

When Jesus was in the Garden of Gethsemane, He told His disciples to watch and pray. Then He went away to pray. The Bible says, "And when He returned, He found them asleep again, for their eyes were heavy; and they did not know what to answer Him."[156] They didn't know "what to answer Him" because they were without excuse. So often we would rather sleep than pray. The spirit is willing, but the flesh is weak. God knows our weaknesses and gave us His Holy Spirit to help us overcome them. So, live in the Spirit. That means that you will have to exercise yourself to godliness. As with physical exercise, this requires a measure of discipline, and it can be sidetracked by excuses. But just as you train your body to reach a specific goal, you have a godly goal!: to reach the lost. Nothing else should matter like that goal. It is your high calling.

There goes another minute.
Gone forever. Go share your faith while you still have time.

TICK ...

Light the Fuse

The world often accuses us of pushing religion "down their throats." Accommodate them. Make sure that you don't push religion down their throats. Instead, give them the Ten Cannons of God's Law. If the Law is allowed to have its way, it won't go down the throat. It will stop the mouth. That's the purpose of the Ten Cannons—to stop every mouth and leave the whole world guilty before God.[157] So, light the fuse. Watch the Law shut the mouth of justification. Let them taste the fear of God. If the use of fear concerns you, ask yourself, which is better—the fear of God in the Day of Grace, which will bring them to the cross, or to have no fear of God right up until the Day of Judgment, which will bring them to the Lake of Fire?

There goes another minute.
Gone forever. **Go share your faith while you still have time.**

TICK ...
TICK ...
TICK ...
TICK ...
TICK ...
TICK ...
TICK ...
TICK ...
TICK ...
TICK ...
TICK ...
TICK ...
TICK ...
TICK ...
TICK ...
TICK ...
TICK ...
TICK ...
TICK ...
TICK ...
TICK ...
TICK ...
TICK ...
TICK ...
TICK ...
TICK ...

Guilt or Joy?

Does the word, "evangelism," evoke a feeling of guilt or joy? Do you run to your evangelistic responsibility as did Philip to the Ethiopian, or do you run from your evangelistic responsibility, as did Jonah? More than likely, the spirit is willing, but the flesh is feeble. Our hearts want to seek and save the lost, but our Adamic natures would far rather stay tucked in the bed of indifference. That's why we need the good alarm clock of a tender conscience. If we *really care* about someone, we will make every effort to witness to him or her. If we don't care, we won't bother. That's why we need God to continually help us to reach the lost. We need a sensitive conscience that will speak to us if we don't care about the lost. So listen to the conscience, and be always led by the Spirit.

There goes another minute.
Gone forever. Go share your faith
while you still have time.

Shout It From the Housetops

How many Bibles do you own? How many sit behind church pews? We have so much light, and yet we keep it to ourselves. We say that we are rich, and yet compared to the Church of the *Book of Acts*, we are poor, blind, wretched, miserable, and naked. We have become so introverted, we have forgotten the meaning of the word, "compassion." Most of us live as monks with a vow of silence when it comes to speaking to the lost. We live in a monastery without walls. Break the vows. Monks in monasteries and vows of silence are for the religious, not for the Christian. We have something to shout from the housetops. We are called to lift up our voices like trumpets, not silence them, and we will not do that unless we go *into* the world and reach out to our sphere of personal influence.

There goes another minute. *Gone forever*. Go share your faith while you still have time.

TICK ...
TICK ...
TICK ...
TICK ...
TICK ...
TICK ...
TICK ...
TICK ...
TICK ...
TICK ...
TICK ...
TICK ...
TICK ...
TICK ...
TICK ...
TICK ...
TICK ...
TICK ...
TICK ...
TICK ...
TICK ...
TICK ...
TICK ...
TICK ...
TICK ...
TICK ...
TICK ...
TICK ...

Witnessing to Moslems

If you witness to a Moslem, realize that he will almost certainly acknowledge his sins, but will trust in God to forgive him because he says that he is sorry, and won't sin again. So, *before* you open up the Law, tell him the story about a criminal who has committed a *very* serious crime. He says, "Judge, I am guilty, but I'm sorry and I won't do it again." Make sure that the Moslem agrees that if the judge is good, he *must* punish the criminal. He would be a bad judge if he didn't make sure justice was done. He cannot simply let him go. Then take the Moslem through the Law, and when he tries to justify himself by saying that he simply asks God to forgive him, remind him of the story you told him about the good judge, and point out that God is infinitely harsher. Then tell him the good news of the cross.

There goes another minute.
Gone forever. Go share your faith
while you still have time.

Scripture's Consistency

Any skeptic could prove the Bible to be supernatural merely by studying any subject from Genesis to Revelation. Take Judgment Day. The Book of Daniel says, "I watched till thrones were put in place, and the Ancient of Days was seated; His garment was white as snow, and the hair of His head was like pure wool. His throne was a fiery flame, its wheels a burning fire; A fiery stream issued and came forth from before Him. A thousand thousands ministered to Him; ten thousand times ten thousand stood before Him. The court was seated, and the books were opened."[158] Seven hundred years later, John described Jesus the same way. He said, "His head and His hair were white like wool, as white as snow, and His eyes like a flame of fire." Paul, adds, "Our God is a consuming fire." What a fearful day that will be.

The Scales of Justice

Unregenerate humanity is "found wanting" on the scales of God's Justice. Yet, to speak of any thought of Judgment Day is offensive to them. They say within their sinful hearts, "God has forgotten: He hides His face; He will never see it"[159] But as surely as God is faithful to all His promises of blessing for the obedient, so is He faithful to His promise of justice for the disobedient. He will fulfill His Word, which He has magnified above His name. The Scriptures warn sinners that in accordance with their hardness and impenitent hearts, they are treasuring up for themselves wrath "in the day of wrath and revelation of the righteous judgment of God, who will render to each one according to his deeds ... to those who are self-seeking and do not obey the truth, but obey unrighteousness—indignation and wrath, tribulation and anguish, on every soul of man who does evil ..."[160]

There goes another minute.
Gone forever. Go share your faith
while you still have time.

Acquainted With Grief

The Apostle Paul had a passion for the lost. He cried, "Necessity is laid upon me!" A "continual, intense distress" was laid upon him. He wasn't a superficial Christian. When sinners conclude a time of witnessing with the patronizing, "Well, I'm pleased you are happy," tell them that you're not "happy." Do you think "happy" would be the right word to use to describe the state of mind of the survivors of the Titanic as they sat in lifeboats with loved ones drowning all around them? They would have unspeakable joy that they were saved, but they would be grieved beyond words at what was happening around them. The Bible says that Jesus had an "oil of gladness above His fellows,"[161] but He was a "Man of sorrows, acquainted with grief."[162] Are you acquainted with the grief of the fate of the lost? It should consume us.

There goes another minute.
Gone forever. **Go share your faith while you still have time.**

TICK ...
TICK ...
TICK ...
TICK ...
TICK ...
TICK ...
TICK ...
TICK ...
TICK ...
TICK ...
TICK ...
TICK ...
TICK ...
TICK ...
TICK ...
TICK ...
TICK ...
TICK ...
TICK ...
TICK ...
TICK ...
TICK ...
TICK ...
TICK ...
TICK ...

The Conflict

Are you grieved to see God's mercy ignored? At the same time, do you cringe in fear for those who have no fear of God before their eyes? Jeremiah had this conflict. He cried, "Oh, that my head were waters, and my eyes a fountain of tears, that I might weep day and night for … my people. Oh that … I might leave my people and go from them! For they are all adulterers, an assembly of treacherous men."[163] Sadly, many professing Christians lack this conflict. They don't know the terror of the Lord and so they don't seek to "persuade men." They have lost contact with the world. Life consists of Saturday night fellowship, Sunday services, Wednesday Bible study, and a few other social activities. They are living in a Christian comfort zone. If this is you, please, break out today.

There goes another minute.
Gone forever. **Go share your faith while you still have time.**

Imitating Paul

The eighth and ninth of the Ten Commandments forbid lying and stealing. Do you ever ask sinners if they have lied or stolen? Paul used the Commandments in Romans chapter two, and he told us to imitate him.[164] When we do that, it shows sinners that they have fallen short of God's standard. The Moral Law reveals that we have sinned against a God who sees every deed and word, and will bring every work into judgment, including every secret thing. The Law of God brings the knowledge of sin. It calls for our blood, and demands our death and damnation. When a sinful world understands that, they are ready for the Good News that Christ redeemed us from the curse of the Law, being made a curse for us. The Law makes the cross make sense. That's why Jesus used it. That's why Paul used it. Do the same.

There goes another minute.
Gone forever. **Go share your faith while you still have time.**

TICK ...
TICK ...
TICK ...
TICK ...
TICK ...
TICK ...
TICK ...
TICK ...
TICK ...
TICK ...
TICK ...
TICK ...
TICK ...
TICK ...
TICK ...
TICK ...
TICK ...
TICK ...
TICK ...
TICK ...
TICK ...
TICK ...
TICK ...
TICK ...
TICK ...
TICK ...

317

Unbending Justice

Recently a man, caught drinking and driving for the eighteenth time, was ordered by a judge to live closer to the liquor store, so that he wouldn't have to drive there. Meanwhile, drunk drivers know that if they are caught, they will only get a rap over the knuckles, even though they are responsible for slaughtering thousands of innocent people on our roads. Some countries have more respect for human life. If you are caught drinking and driving in South Africa, you get a ten-year prison sentence and a $10,000 fine. Sweden will give you an automatic jail sentence and one year of hard labor. Bulgaria will execute you on your second offense. El Salvador will make sure you don't drink and drive again. They will execute you by firing squad on your first offense. God's justice will also be unbending on the Day of Judgment. There will be no second chance.

There goes another minute.
Gone forever. **Go share your faith while you still have time.**

Pained at the Heart

God's Justice will be so thorough of Judgment Day, sinners will be "ground to powder." David cried, "Horror has taken hold on me because of the wicked who forsake Your Law."[165] J. Oswald Sanders pleaded in prayer, "Give us souls, lest we die!" Jeremiah cried, "My bowels, my bowels! I am pained at my very heart, my heart makes a noise in me, I cannot hold my peace, because you have heard. Oh my soul, the sound of the trumpet, the alarm of war."[166] Charles Haddon Spurgeon said, "When I've shot and spent all my Gospel bullets and have none left and little effect seems to be made upon my hearers, I then get in the gun and shoot myself at them." In other words, when he had preached the truth of God's Word, his burden was such that he opened his own heart and simply implored sinners to come to the Savior.

There goes another minute.
Gone forever. Go share your faith
while you still have time.

TICK ...
TICK ...
TICK ...
TICK ...
TICK ...
TICK ...
TICK ...
TICK ...
TICK ...
TICK ...
TICK ...
TICK ...
TICK ...
TICK ...
TICK ...
TICK ...
TICK ...
TICK ...
TICK ...
TICK ...
TICK ...
TICK ...
TICK ...
TICK ...
TICK ...
TICK ...
TICK ...

319

Would We Empty a Pen?

Joseph Alleine, a puritan of the 16th Century, wrote a book called, *Alarm to the Unconverted*. In it, his zeal for the unconverted is very evident. Listen to his heart as he prepares to plead with the sinner: "But from whence shall I fetch my argument? With what shall I win them? Oh, that I could tell! I would write to them in tears, I would weep out every argument, I would empty my veins for ink, I would petition them on my knees. Oh how thankful I would be if they would be prevailed with to repent and turn." Listen to his concern for the lost— "I would empty my veins for ink." How many of us would empty a pen of ink, **let alone blood,** to warn a loved one or a friend to get right with God? Show that you care. Use today to reach out to the unsaved.

There goes another minute. *Gone forever*. Go share your faith while you still have time.

The Two Drunks

Two drunks walked along a wharf one dark night, climbed into a small boat, and determined to row to the other side of the lake. The first drunk rowed for one and a half hours. Sweat poured from his brow until he collapsed. The second drunk took the oars and rowed for three hours. He collapsed, exhausted. When they awoke at sunrise, they found that they had made only one mistake. *They were still tied to the wharf.* Are you still tied to the wharf of self-will? Is the Christian life one of labor and sorrow? Is it one of struggle, sweat, and misery? Then it may be that you have never cut the ropes from the wharf of self-will. Today, abandon yourself to a faithful Creator. Don't wait any longer! Pull out the pin of self-will, and then place yourself as a grenade into the Hand of Almighty God.

There goes another minute.
Gone forever. **Go share your faith while you still have time.**

TICK ...
TICK ...
TICK ...
TICK ...
TICK ...
TICK ...
TICK ...
TICK ...
TICK ...
TICK ...
TICK ...
TICK ...
TICK ...
TICK ...
TICK ...
TICK ...
TICK ...
TICK ...
TICK ...
TICK ...
TICK ...
TICK ...
TICK ...
TICK ...
TICK ...
TICK ...

Self Discipline

Have you discovered the key to being successful as a Christian? Of course, we don't measure "success" in dollars as the world does. We measure it in terms of our life being pleasing to God. The key is self-discipline to the words of Jesus. He said that if we continue in His word, we are His disciples indeed, and the result will be that we will know the truth, and that will give us freedom.[167] Self-discipline means self-denial. It means listening to the voice of your conscience and the voice of the Holy Spirit. Consider Jesus. His ministry was a complete denial of self, from the temptation in the wilderness to Calvary's terrible cross. He denied His own will and disciplined Himself to the will of the Father for the love of God and mankind. So, make sure you are a disciple today— that you are disciplined to do the will of God.

There goes another minute. *Gone forever.* Go share your faith while you still have time.

Afraid of Failure

Are you afraid of failure? Perhaps you have had a bad witnessing experience. Maybe you embarrassed yourself because you didn't know what to say. Or perhaps someone discouraged you from sharing your faith. Don't let the past stop you from reaching out to the unsaved in the future. *Learn* from your mistakes. Study more. Pray more. Trust God more. The only failure is a failure to be faithful to God. Those who blunder the least are usually those who attempt the least. Steven Pile, the head of the "Not Terribly Good Club" of Great Britain, was forced to resign from his position when a book he wrote called, *The Book of Heroic Failures*, became a bestseller. He failed as a failure. Albert Einstein said, "Anyone who has never made a mistake has never tried anything new." So, do what the Bible says—forget that which is behind.

There goes another minute.
Gone forever. **Go share your faith while you still have time.**

TICK ...
TICK ...
TICK ...
TICK ...
TICK ...
TICK ...
TICK ...
TICK ...
TICK ...
TICK ...
TICK ...
TICK ...
TICK ...
TICK ...
TICK ...
TICK ...
TICK ...
TICK ...
TICK ...
TICK ...
TICK ...
TICK ...
TICK ...
TICK ...
TICK ...
TICK ...

323

Careful When Gathering Sticks

A young man wondered if he should go to a Bible school. His business was carpet-cleaning. Because he traveled around, he personally witnessed to six or seven people each day. His future at a mission school would mean that he would spend six months with Christians. Then he would go out and do mission work ... if he still had a mind to. Charles Spurgeon said, "Be careful when you are picking up sticks, that your fire doesn't go out." So if you are considering going to a Bible school, make sure they have an emphasis on reaching out to the world, so that you will end up with more zeal than when you enrolled. Better still, get into a lifestyle where you will be schooled by regularly rubbing shoulders with the world.

**There goes another minute.
Gone forever. Go share your faith
while you still have time.**

Getaway Time

Airports are wonderful places to reach the unsaved. Where else in today's busy world can you find people, sitting and doing nothing? We have tracts that are excellent for airports.[168] One in particular is called the "Intelligence Test Bookmark." It doesn't look at all like a Christian tract, and gives plenty of time to get away. Its heading boosts the ego by saying, "Intelligence Test … for the thinking mind." Below the heading are eight brainteasers. Number seven asks a question about a man who had broken the Ten Commandments. When he made it to the gates of Heaven, he found that God was "just," and by His very nature, had to punish sin. How could God let him into Heaven and still be just? On side two, it gives all the answers, including an explanation of how God did it through the cross.

There goes another minute.
Gone forever. Go share your faith
while you still have time.

TICK ...
TICK ...
TICK ...
TICK ...
TICK ...
TICK ...
TICK ...
TICK ...
TICK ...
TICK ...
TICK ...
TICK ...
TICK ...
TICK ...
TICK ...
TICK ...
TICK ...
TICK ...
TICK ...
TICK ...
TICK ...
TICK ...
TICK ...
TICK ...
TICK ...
TICK ...

325

The Widow's Mite

Are you grateful for Calvary? Do you look at the cross with tears in your eyes? Then show God your gratitude. Give Him the "widow's mite" of your evangelistic witness. The incident of the poor widow giving her last two coins to God shows us that only the gift that costs, counts. God knows what it costs you to stand up for the Gospel. Perhaps for you to give a tract to an unsaved person may be equivalent (on a "courage level") to some other Christian standing up and preaching in the open air. Don't let fear stop you. *You can do it.* Don't listen to your fears. Say, "If God is for me, nothing can be against me. I can do all things through Christ who strengthens me." Then do it. Civil law is still on our side—you'll not be thrown to the lions. Let the devil eat dust.

There goes another minute.
Gone forever. **Go share your faith while you still have time.**

The Spirit of the Law

There is a movie called, "The Fourth Wise Man." It's about a man who truly loved God. When he and his servant came across a stricken stranger, they bathed his wounds, and when they had to leave, he said to his servant, "Leave him with sufficient bread and water." When the servant protested, "There is hardly any left," he said, "Leave all of it then." The servant was saying that there was barely enough to keep *them* alive, and was no doubt hoping his master would say not to leave any, or at least only leave the minimum. But this man did to others as he would have them do to him, fulfilling the Law and the prophets. Such acts of kindness don't come naturally to us, but with the help of God, we can express our love for the lost in that spirit.

**There goes another minute.
Gone forever. Go share your faith
while you still have time.**

God's Delight

"Thus says the Lord, 'Let not the wise man glory in his wisdom, neither let the mighty man glory in his might, let not the rich man glory in his riches: But let him that glories glory in this, that he understands and knows me, that I am the Lord which exercise lovingkindness, judgment, and righteousness, in the earth: for in these things I delight, saith the Lord.'"[169] We may have the wisdom of Solomon, the might of Samson, or the riches of Abraham, but God says that that is nothing to get excited about. We should instead be rejoicing if we know God and understand what it is that pleases Him. He *delights* in lovingkindness, judgment, and righteousness. And there is no greater evidence of these things than in the cross of Calvary. It was there that He once and for all displayed His love, His justice, and His righteousness.

There goes another minute.
Gone forever. **Go share your faith while you still have time.**

Along the left margin, repeated: TICK ...

The Wisdom From Above

The Bible says of Moses, he "was learned in all the wisdom of the Egyptians, and was mighty in words, and deeds"[170] yet God didn't use him to deliver Israel until 40 years later. It took all that time of tending sheep to produce a meekness of character different from that which he had in Egypt. The wisdom that Moses gained from Egypt was not the wisdom from above. When he saw injustice, he took the law into his own hands and committed murder.[171] God doesn't want us to have the shallow wisdom of this world. Instead, He wants a humble, peace-loving, compassionate character to use as a mouthpiece for the Gospel. That's what we can have in Christ. We don't need to tend sheep for 40 years when we have the character of the Good Shepherd manifesting through us.

There goes another minute.
Gone forever. **Go share your faith while you still have time.**

TICK ...
TICK ...
TICK ...
TICK ...
TICK ...
TICK ...
TICK ...
TICK ...
TICK ...
TICK ...
TICK ...
TICK ...
TICK ...
TICK ...
TICK ...
TICK ...
TICK ...
TICK ...
TICK ...
TICK ...
TICK ...
TICK ...
TICK ...
TICK ...
TICK ...
TICK ...
TICK ...

Wasted From
One End to the Other

Just before his death at the age of 85, Louis Aragon, one of France's greatest poets, described his life as "an awesome gamble which I have lost and wasted from one end to the other." Don't be like him. Spend your time seeking the lost by witnessing whenever and wherever you can. In doing so, you will make sure you are in the perfect will of God. Don't wait for Him to especially speak to you about when and where you should witness. He has already told you to do it. He has commanded us to go into all the world and preach to every creature. We are commanded to preach the word "in season and out of season."[172] So, if you can't find someone to speak to, go to a mall, sit on a seat, and simply pray that God will bring someone to you. You won't have to wait too long.

There goes another minute.
Gone forever. **Go share your faith**
while you still have time.

Faith in God

Some people say that they find it difficult to have faith in God. But there's a difference between having faith that *there is* a God and having faith *in* God. It doesn't take much faith to believe that God exists. Creation proves that there's a Creator in the same way a building proves that there was a builder, or a painting that there's a painter. A child can have that sort of faith. However, faith *in* God means to "trust" Him, and it is through that trust that we receive the gift of everlasting life. It's as though we were sinking into a deep black hole that is filling with water. God kindly lowers the "rope" of the Savior and pulls us out, and He now has trusted us to work with Him to persuade the world to take hold of the Savior.

There goes another minute.
Gone forever. Go share your faith
while you still have time.

We Can Only Recreate

All around us we see the genius of God's creative hand—beautiful flowers, amazing birds, tall trees, the magnificence of the sun, the moon, the stars, etc., every one of which is far more complex than anything that man has made. Actually, man hasn't really "made" anything. Ask our most intelligent scientist if he can make you something from nothing—a flower, a tree, or maybe a bird—from nothing. We don't know how to "make" a grain of sand. We can recreate, but we have no idea how to create. So, if modern man with all his genius cannot create a grain of sand from nothing, how dare he imagine in his wildest dreams that this incredibly complex creation, of which we are part, came into being without a Maker? Such thoughts are intellectual suicide.

There goes another minute. *Gone forever.* **Go share your faith while you still have time.**

TICK ...
TICK ...
TICK ...
TICK ...
TICK ...
TICK ...
TICK ...
TICK ...
TICK ...
TICK ...
TICK ...
TICK ...
TICK ...
TICK ...
TICK ...
TICK ...
TICK ...
TICK ...
TICK ...
TICK ...
TICK ...
TICK ...
TICK ...
TICK ...
TICK ...

Friendly Fire

"Friendly fire" is the army's way of saying that they accidentally killed their own troops. It's an absurd expression. There is nothing "friendly" about being shot in the back by your own side. Whatever it's called, to kill someone in your own army is to do the work of the enemy. Early in 1997, a 26-year old man was the subject of gossip in his church in Costa Mesa, California. He was said to be a nice young man with a friendly disposition, but the incessant gossip was too much for him. He hung himself. His suicide note said, "Gossip kills." He was a victim of friendly fire. Think of his parents' pain. Think of the guilt of those who spread the gossip. Think of the testimony of a church, and always think before you lend your tongue to demons and spread poison. Instead, spread the Gospel.

There goes another minute.
Gone forever. **Go share your faith while you still have time.**

TICK ...
TICK ...
TICK ...
TICK ...
TICK ...
TICK ...
TICK ...
TICK ...
TICK ...
TICK ...
TICK ...
TICK ...
TICK ...
TICK ...
TICK ...
TICK ...
TICK ...
TICK ...
TICK ...
TICK ...
TICK ...
TICK ...
TICK ...
TICK ...
TICK ...
TICK ...
TICK ...
TICK ...

333

Unity in the Body

We are told in Scripture to "stand fast in one spirit, with one mind striving together for the faith of the Gospel."[173] Some years ago at the Seattle Special Olympics, nine contestants, all physically or mentally disabled, lined up for the 100-yard race. When the starting gun fired, they took off with a relish to run the race to the finish and win. All, that is, except for one boy who stumbled, fell over and began to cry. The other eight heard the boy cry, slowed down, and looked back. They all turned around and went back. *Every one of them.* One girl with Down's syndrome bent down and kissed him and said, "This will make it better." All nine linked arms and walked across the finish line together. Everyone in the stadium stood, and the cheering went on for several minutes. Striving together for the faith of the Gospel receives Heaven's acclamation.

There goes another minute.
Gone forever. **Go share your faith**
while you still have time.

334

Not Yet Dead

In mid-1993, a 4-year old girl was rushed to a hospital, but arrived clinically dead. Doctors immediately began emergency procedures. After 20 minutes, a special emergency team of ten people was called in. After an incredible 41 minutes of CPR, the little girl's heart began beating again. The doctors didn't give up because they could see that the child's pupils were still responding to light. That meant that the brain was not yet dead. Death has seized upon the sinner. He may seem brain dead, but never give up on witnessing to him. Simply keep applying the pressure of the Law upon his ceased heart. Remember, you are working with a team of ten, and the Scriptures tell us that "the Commandment is a lamp and the Law is light."[174] So, watch the pupils to see if there is response to the light. Let that give you hope.

There goes another minute.
Gone forever. Go share your faith
while you still have time.

The Lost State of the Lost

Those of us who know the Lord tend to take for granted that we have purpose in our existence, and that can make us forget the lost state of the unsaved. Ernest Hemingway said, "Life is a dirty trick, a short journey from nothingness to nothingness." He tragically committed suicide. Henry Longfellow wrote, "Life is but an empty dream," while Samuel Butler said, "Life is just a long process of getting tired." Samuel Becket said, "Life is an indefinite waiting for an explanation that never comes." And that explanation will never come until a sinner comes to the Savior. What an absolute tragedy that people could be alive and yet not know why they are alive. Such knowledge of how lost these poor people are should drive us to our knees that God would have mercy on them and draw them to the Savior before death seizes on them and drags them to Hell.

There goes another minute.
Gone forever. **Go share your faith while you still have time.**

TICK ... TICK ...

The Motivation

In Mark 10:17, a man came running to Jesus, knelt before Him, and asked how he could obtain everlasting life. This man came *running* and *knelt* before the Savior. It would seem that his earnest and humble heart made him a prime candidate as a potential convert. Yet, Jesus didn't give him the message of God's grace. He didn't even mention the love of God. Neither did He tell him of an abundant, wonderful, new life. Instead, Jesus used the Law of God to expose the man's hidden sin. This man was a transgressor of the First of the Ten Commandments. His money was his god, and one cannot serve both God and money. Then the Scriptures reveal that it was *love* that motivated Jesus to speak in this way. We are told, "Then Jesus beholding him loved him."[175] Do we look at this sinful and rebellious world, and love them?

There goes another minute.
Gone forever. Go share your faith
while you still have time.

TICK ...
TICK ...
TICK ...
TICK ...
TICK ...
TICK ...
TICK ...
TICK ...
TICK ...
TICK ...
TICK ...
TICK ...
TICK ...
TICK ...
TICK ...
TICK ...
TICK ...
TICK ...
TICK ...
TICK ...
TICK ...
TICK ...
TICK ...
TICK ...
TICK ...
TICK ...
TICK ...

Driven By Love

John Wesley said, "The second use [of the Law] is to bring him unto life ... it acts the part of a severe schoolmaster. *It drives us by force, rather than draws us by love. And yet, love is the spring of all. It is the spirit of love which, by this painful means, tears away our confidence in the flesh, which leaves us no broken reed whereon to trust, and so constrains the sinner, stripped of all to cry out in the bitterness of his soul or groan in the depth of his heart, 'I give up every plea beside, Lord, I am damned; but thou hast died.'"* How true are his words. When we warn of Hell, we do so because we love them. When we point sinners to the cross, we do so because we love them and are not willing that they perish.

**There goes another minute.
Gone forever. Go share your faith
while you still have time.**

How Do You Feel?

How do you feel when you read these words?
"And if your hand makes you sin, cut it off. It
is better for you to enter into life maimed, than
having two hands, to go to Hell, into the fire
that shall never be quenched where 'their worm
does not die and the fire is not quenched.' And
if your foot makes you sin, cut it off. It is better
for you to enter life lame, than having two feet,
to be cast into Hell, into the fire that shall never
be quenched where 'their worm does not die
and the fire is not quenched.' And if your eye
makes you sin, pluck it out. It is better for you
to enter the kingdom of God with one eye, than
having two eyes, to be cast into Hell fire … "[176]
Does it horrify you that that is where the
ungodly are headed?

There goes another minute.
Gone forever. Go share your faith
while you still have time.

Fly on the Wall

Wouldn't you like to have been a fly on the wall of the tomb of Lazarus? The Bible says that when Jesus stood outside the tomb of the four-day's dead man, "He cried with a loud voice, 'Lazarus, come forth!'" Suddenly, there was a stirring from the bound body of the brother of Mary and Martha. He stood to his feet and came out of the tomb. Death had no choice but to leave his body. This was the same voice that in the beginning said, "Let there be light," and light came into being. This was the same voice that calmed the storm on the sea of Galilee, and this is the same voice that said, "I am the resurrection, and the life: he that believeth on me, though he die, yet shall he live; and whosoever lives and believeth on me shall never die."[177] He is the only hope for humanity.

**There goes another minute.
Gone forever. Go share your faith
while you still have time.**

TICK ...
TICK ...
TICK ...
TICK ...
TICK ...
TICK ...
TICK ...
TICK ...
TICK ...
TICK ...
TICK ...
TICK ...
TICK ...
TICK ...
TICK ...
TICK ...
TICK ...
TICK ...
TICK ...
TICK ...
TICK ...
TICK ...
TICK ...
TICK ...
TICK ...
TICK ...

Biblical Evangelism

To what was Jesus referring when He said not
to give what is holy to the dogs? To what was
He pointing when He said not to cast pearls
before swine, lest they trample them under their
feet, and turn and tear you in pieces?[178] The most
precious pearl the Church has is "Christ
crucified." Preach grace to the proud and watch
what they do with it. They will trample the
blood of the Savior under their feet with their
false profession, and, what's more, they will
become enemies of the Gospel. If not physically,
you can be sure they will tear you in pieces
verbally. They have "insulted the Spirit of
grace."[179] That means they insult the Holy
Spirit. "Bitterness" and "backslider" are bad
bedfellows for the Church. The proselyte
becomes a twofold child of Hell. Remember,
biblical evangelism is "Law to the Proud, and
Grace to the Humble."

There goes another minute.
Gone forever. **Go share your faith
while you still have time.**

The Subtlety of Idolatry

We need to beware of the sin of idolatry. When a sinner creates a god in his mind, it opens the door to unrestrained sin. It is fashioned so as to not stir his conscience. His god is a god who has no moral dictates or threats of judgment. A. W. Tozer wrote, "God's justice stands forever against the sinner in utter severity. The vague and tenuous hope that God is too kind to punish the ungodly has become a deadly opiate for the consciences of millions. It hushes their fears and allows them to practice all pleasant forms of iniquity while death draws every day nearer and the command to repent goes unregarded. As responsible moral beings, we dare not so trifle with our eternal future."[180] After John wrote, "This is the true God, and eternal life," he warned "Little children, keep yourselves from idols."[181]

There goes another minute. *Gone forever.* Go share your faith while you still have time.

TICK ... TICK ...

The Agony of the Cross

When commenting on the agony of the cross, Charles Spurgeon said: "The placing of the cross in its socket had shaken Him with great violence, had strained all the ligaments, pained every nerve, and more or less dislocated all His bones. Burdened with His own weight, the august sufferer felt the strain increasing every moment of those six long hours. His sense of faintness and general weakness were overpowering; while to His own consciousness He became nothing but a mass of misery and swooning sickness ... To us, sensations such as our Lord endured would have been insupportable, and kind unconsciousness would have come to our rescue; but in His case, He was wounded, and felt the sword; He drained the cup and tasted every drop." How great must be His love for justice, that He would do such a thing, and how great must His love be for this sinful world.

There goes another minute.
Gone forever. Go share your faith
while you still have time.

The Place of Apologetics

While apologetics (defenses of the faith) play an important part in evangelism, it's vital to realize that they have a limited function in reaching the lost. If we confine our witness to arguing about the existence of God, the inspiration of Scripture, the age of the earth, etc., we are like a man who goes fishing with bait, but no hook. While he may attract the fish, they will end up fat and happy ... and they will get away. The function of bait is to attract the fish and disguise the hook. When the fish come around, the fisherman pulls the hook into the jaw, and catches his fish. Apologetics are the bait, and the hook is God's Law. It is the Law that addresses a man's conscience and brings the knowledge of sin. So, don't spend too much time fishing in the intellect. Do what Jesus did—go for the conscience.

There goes another minute.
Gone forever. Go share your faith
while you still have time.

TICK ...
TICK ...
TICK ...
TICK ...
TICK ...
TICK ...
TICK ...
TICK ...
TICK ...
TICK ...
TICK ...
TICK ...
TICK ...
TICK ...
TICK ...
TICK ...
TICK ...
TICK ...
TICK ...
TICK ...
TICK ...
TICK ...
TICK ...
TICK ...
TICK ...
TICK ...

An Extension Led

Think of the Law as an extension led that is plugged into the power of Heaven. The Gospel is like a light bulb. It is dead without the Law, in that by itself, it gives no light to the darkened mind of a sinful world. Their understanding is "darkened, being alienated from the life of God through the ignorance that is in them because of the blindness of their heart."[182] However, once the Gospel is connected to the Law, it becomes the power of God to salvation. This was the case with the Jews on the Day of Pentecost, with Nathaniel, and with Nicodemus. Until the Law gives the light of understanding, the cross is foolishness to a world that sits in darkness. The god of this world has blinded their minds "lest the light of the glorious Gospel of Christ, who is the image of God, should shine unto them."[183]

There goes another minute.
Gone forever. Go share your faith
while you still have time.

The Spade That Turns the Soil

The key to reaching the lost is the evangelistic use of the Law of God. It is the key that unlocks the door of the Savior. It is the spade that turns the soils and prepares it for the seed of the Gospel. Look at the description of the function of the Law in *Pilgrim's Progress*: "It was he [the Law] who did bind my heavy burden upon me." Faithful agrees: "Aye. Had it not been for him, we had both of us stayed in the City of Destruction." "Then he did us a favor," answered Christian. [Faithful then shows how the Law alarms us:] "Aye. Albeit, he did it none too gently." Then Christian says, "Well, at least he played the part of a schoolmaster and showed us our need. It was he who drove us to the cross."

There goes another minute.
Gone forever. **Go share your faith**
while you still have time.

Chicken Wings

A farmer once looked at what was left of his farm after a forest fire had destroyed everything. Dead chickens lay on the ground, unable to escape the fast-moving, ravaging flames. He bent down and picked up a dead chicken, and to his amazement found a number of chicks sheltering under the wings of their mother. She had instinctively spread her wings to save her beloved offspring. That's what God did for us in Jesus Christ. Jesus likened the love of God to a chicken gathering her chicks under her wings.[184] It is there that we receive shelter from the devouring flames of the wrath of a holy God. It is in the shelter of the wings of mercy that we are safe from the fury of Eternal Justice. May we never forget such love, and may it spur us to reach out to this world before they face the fire of His wrath.

**There goes another minute.
Gone forever. Go share your faith
while you still have time.**

The Universal Call

Listen to the Bible's universal call to all humanity: "Look to Me, and be saved, *all you ends of the earth!*"[185] Jesus said, "Therefore go into the highways, and *as many as you find,* invite to the wedding."[186] The Bible also says, "Jesus stood and cried out, saying, 'If *anyone* thirsts, let him come to Me and drink.'"[187] Paul, in writing to Timothy, said, "[God] desires all men to be saved and to come to the knowledge of the truth."[188] And John makes it clear who salvation is for by saying, "And the Spirit and the bride say, 'Come!' And let him who hears say, 'Come!' And let him who thirsts come. And *whoever* desires, let him take the water of life freely."[189] So that means we can, with confidence, go into all the world and preach the Gospel to *every* creature.

There goes another minute. *Gone forever*. Go share your faith while you still have time.

The Imagination

The imagination is a wonderful gift of God that can give you images before you create something, but if it is allowed, it will carry you into shameful sin. The Book of Genesis tells us that the reason God destroyed the entire human race, except for eight people, was that "the imagination of man's heart is evil from his youth."[190] One of the things that God hates is "a heart that devises wicked imaginations."[191] When God pointed Ezekiel to the sin of Israel, He said, "Son of man, have you seen what the ancients of the house of Israel do in the dark, every man in the chambers of his imagery?"[192] The key to a good imagination is to line the walls of the mind with the fear of God, and then to use that gift of God for the extension of His Kingdom and for the glory of His name.

TICK ...
TICK ...
TICK ...
TICK ...
TICK ...
TICK ...
TICK ...
TICK ...
TICK ...
TICK ...
TICK ...
TICK ...
TICK ...
TICK ...
TICK ...
TICK ...
TICK ...
TICK ...
TICK ...
TICK ...
TICK ...
TICK ...
TICK ...
TICK ...
TICK ...
TICK ...

349

The Great Giant

In C. S. Lewis' famous book, *The Lion, the Witch and the Wardrobe*, Aslan is about to turn a great giant back from stone to being alive once again. As he is ready to breathe on the giant's feet, he says, "Once the feet are put right, all the rest of him will follow." How true that is of the Church. It is stony-hearted when it comes to reaching out to the lost, and when it loses the Gospel influence, it becomes good for nothing but to be trampled underfoot by men. We need the Lion of the Tribe of Judah to breathe on the Church so that its feet will be shod with the preparation of the Gospel of Peace. It's then that the Bible says its feet will become beautiful.[193] Once the feet are right, all the rest of the Body of Christ will stand up and be the giant it is supposed to be.

There goes another minute. *Gone forever*. Go share your faith while you still have time.

Dirt Shirts

Do you get upset when you see someone in a mall wearing an offensive T-shirt? Do you feel disgusted by their flagrant rebellion against what they know is right? Then take courage and warmly greet then, and give them a Gospel tract. Often, people who wear filthy shirts are avoided by other people, and it almost shocks them when someone shows them kindness. More than likely, they will politely accept the tract. Another reason we shouldn't hesitate to approach this type of person is that their apparel shows that they don't care what people think, and therefore they may be the boldest of witnesses for the Gospel. Besides, some of the cleanest, well-dressed, and approachable people may not have dirt on their shirts, but they sure have dirt in their hearts.

There goes another minute.
Gone forever. Go share your faith
while you still have time.

TICK ... TICK ... TICK ... TICK

You're running out of time, and you're also
running out of devotional pages.
A whole year has nearly passed!

Order *The Way of the Master Minute, Book 2*
today! Either stop by your local Christian
bookstore or go online at
www.WayoftheMaster.com.

The Works That Follow

When the richest man on earth dies, how much money do you think that he will leave behind? The answer is, "All of it." Isn't it ironic? The man may be able to buy anything he wants in this world. But he won't take a thing with him. Not a bean. But Christians *can* take something with them—their good works. The Bible says that they "follow" us. The Bible says "And I heard a voice from heaven saying to me, Write, Blessed are the dead which die in the Lord from henceforth: Yes, says the Spirit, that they may rest from their labors; *and their works do follow them.*"[194] Because of the cross, God no longer sees good works as an attempt to bribe Him to forgive our sins. They instead flow from gratitude, and are acceptable to Him. The greatest good work we can do is to seek the souls for whom He died.

There goes another minute. *Gone forever.* Go share your faith while you still have time.

TICK ...
TICK ...
TICK ...
TICK ...
TICK ...
TICK ...
TICK ...
TICK ...
TICK ...
TICK ...
TICK ...
TICK ...
TICK ...
TICK ...
TICK ...
TICK ...
TICK ...
TICK ...
TICK ...
TICK ...
TICK ...
TICK ...
TICK ...
TICK ...
TICK ...
TICK ...
TICK ...

Eternal Seeds

If you found yourself on a plane that was going to crash when its fuel ran out, would you, *could* you stand up and preach? Would you be prepared for such a time? Do you have a clear five-minute Gospel message ready? Do you have a two-minute Gospel message, so that you are ready to share with someone who is waiting of a bus? How about for when you hear, "Sorry, wrong number."? Are you ready to say a quick, "Make sure you read your Bible."? If the person says, "Excuse me?", be ready to repeat, "Make sure you read your Bible. There's nothing more important than your eternal salvation." You can also say this when ordering something over the phone. When the operator finishes with "Is there anything else I can do for you?" say, "Yes, please. Make sure you read your Bible." Be bold. Plant a seed for eternity.

There goes another minute.
Gone forever. **Go share your faith while you still have time.**

TICK ...
TICK ...
TICK ...
TICK ...
TICK ...
TICK ...
TICK ...
TICK ...
TICK ...
TICK ...
TICK ...
TICK ...
TICK ...
TICK ...
TICK ...
TICK ...
TICK ...
TICK ...
TICK ...
TICK ...
TICK ...
TICK ...
TICK ...
TICK ...
TICK ...

To Exist or Not To Exist

"I am" is not only the shortest complete sentence in the English language, it is the closest the English language has for the name of God. When God appeared to Moses, He said, "I AM THAT I AM: and he said, Thus shall you say to the children of Israel, I AM has sent me to you."[195] We are made in the image of I AM. We know that "we are." Mankind has the unique knowledge that "he is." We are human "beings" and the fact that we are beings means that we are aware of our existence. We also know that death awaits us. When Macbeth was contemplating suicide, he said, "To *be*, or not to *be*, that is the question." Sadly, the ungodly think that they will cease to "be" after death, but they will continue to "be" throughout eternity. Death isn't the termination of existence.

There goes another minute.
Gone forever. **Go share your faith while you still have time.**

The Jawbone of a Donkey

The Bible tells us that Samson was bound with ropes, but "the Spirit of the Lord came mightily upon him; and the ropes that were on his arms became like flax that is burned with fire ... He found a fresh jawbone of a donkey, reached out his hand and took it, and killed a thousand men with it."[196] Has the enemy bound you with the ropes of the fear of man? Then realize that God is looking for jawbones of donkeys. He wants to speak through lowly creatures of burden. God spoke through a donkey to Balaam and He can speak though you. Let the Spirit of God come upon you today and break the restraints. Give Him your jawbone. A lowly and faithful donkey carried the Savior into Jerusalem, and that is your humble task today—to take Jesus to this lost and dying world.

There goes another minute.
Gone forever. Go share your faith
while you still have time.

TICK ...
TICK ...
TICK ...
TICK ...
TICK ...
TICK ...
TICK ...
TICK ...
TICK ...
TICK ...
TICK ...
TICK ...
TICK ...
TICK ...
TICK ...
TICK ...
TICK ...
TICK ...
TICK ...
TICK ...
TICK ...
TICK ...
TICK ...
TICK ...
TICK ...
TICK ...
TICK ...

355

At War With the Law

Look at how Charles Spurgeon used God's Law to make sinners see that they needed the Savior. "Soul! You will find it a hard thing to go at war with the Law. When the Law came in peace, Sinai was altogether on a smoke, and even Moses said, I exceedingly fear and quake. What will you do when the Law comes in terror? When the trumpet of the archangel shall tear you from your grave. When the eyes of God shall burn their way into your guilty soul. When the great books shall be opened and all your sin and shame shall be punished. Can you stand against an angry Law in that day?" Compare that to today's sermons where words are carefully chosen so that the sinner won't be alarmed or feel any guilt. Yet, that's what they must feel, or they will never come to the foot of the cross.

There goes another minute.
Gone forever. Go share your faith
while you still have time.

The Waiter

Watch how a waiter comes to your table at a restaurant. When he interrupts your conversation and asks if you are ready to order, you don't say, "Excuse me! I was talking with my friend and you butted in. You are very rude!" This is because he has something that you want. Food. That's why he is confident. We have something that the world wants. Everlasting life. There is a cry within the heart of every sane human being that says, "I don't want to die!" And it's that knowledge that gives us our confidence. Notice what happens if a new waiter is shy. He is put with an experienced waiter, and when he sees that people aren't offended when he butts in, his confidence builds. So, go with an experienced waiter. Watch Paul's boldness in Romans 2, or watch Jesus in Mark 10, and watch your own confidence grow.

There goes another minute.
Gone forever. Go share your faith
while you still have time.

Had He Been in Prayer

Jesus warned Peter that he would deny Him, and then Jesus and His disciples went to the Garden of Gethsemane to pray. Peter fell asleep when he should have been praying. Had he been prayerful, he might have been faithful. Had he been prayerful, he might not have used his sword to cut off the ear of the servant of the high priest. Had he been in prayer in the garden, he might not have followed Jesus "afar off." Had he been in prayer, he might not have denied his Lord when a young maiden asked if he knew Him. It's our time in prayer that keeps us from following the dictates of the flesh. It's our time in prayer that keeps us close to Jesus. And it's our time in prayer that helps keep us from being ashamed of the One who suffered and died for us.

**There goes another minute.
Gone forever. Go share your faith
while you still have time.**

TICK ...
TICK ...
TICK ...
TICK ...
TICK ...
TICK ...
TICK ...
TICK ...
TICK ...
TICK ...
TICK ...
TICK ...
TICK ...
TICK ...
TICK ...
TICK ...
TICK ...
TICK ...
TICK ...
TICK ...
TICK ...
TICK ...
TICK ...
TICK ...

The Bitter Made Sweet

The Scriptures say that Moses led Israel into the wilderness, where they became very thirsty. But when they came to Marah and found water, they couldn't drink because it was bitter.[197] He then cast a tree into the waters and they became sweet. Moses can only lead sinners into the wilderness and bitterness of death. They are left thirsting for righteousness. Paul said, "And the commandment, which was ordained to life, I found to be unto death."[198] The Law seems a bitter thing, until the tree is thrown into the mix. It is the wooden cross that shows the Law to be what it is — the "Schoolmaster that brings us to Christ." That's why Paul concluded, "the Law is holy, and the commandment holy, and just, and good."[199] So let the Law do its work before you preach the cross, and watch the bitter suddenly become sweet.

There goes another minute.
Gone forever. Go share your faith
while you still have time.

TICK ...
TICK ...
TICK ...
TICK ...
TICK ...
TICK ...
TICK ...
TICK ...
TICK ...
TICK ...
TICK ...
TICK ...
TICK ...
TICK ...
TICK ...
TICK ...
TICK ...
TICK ...
TICK ...
TICK ...
TICK ...
TICK ...
TICK ...
TICK ...
TICK ...
TICK ...
TICK ...
TICK ...
TICK ...

The Everlasting Gospel

Look at how Scripture exalts the Gospel: "And I saw another angel fly in the midst of heaven, having the everlasting Gospel to preach to them that dwell on the earth ..."[200] The Gospel that you have been commanded to preach is called "the *everlasting* Gospel." Think of it. You have the incredible privilege of preaching the everlasting Gospel in the last days. What an honor— to preach Christ crucified. Let it sink into your mind— God has given you words of everlasting life to give to dying sinners. The Bible says: "And many of them that sleep in the dust of the earth shall awake, some to everlasting life, and some to shame and everlasting contempt. And they that be wise shall shine as the brightness of the firmament; and they that turn many to righteousness as the stars for ever and ever."[201]

**There goes another minute.
Gone forever. Go share your faith
while you still have time.**

The Sound Man

While some may think that the most difficult job in the church is to be the pastor, there is one other job that isn't easy. It is the job of the sound man. No one knows that he even exists until something goes wrong with the sound. Suddenly, when there's an annoying "buzz," everyone looks around at the sound man. That's often the way it is with God. The world doesn't think about God until things go wrong. They take the blessings of life for granted. While tragedies sometimes make an opening for the Gospel, it's not always the case. Some people become bitter at God when life throws them a curve ball. So, don't fall into the trap of waiting for bad things to happen to the unsaved, before you try to share the Gospel with them. The Bible says, "Now is the day of salvation."[202]

There goes another minute. _Gone forever_. Go share your faith while you still have time.

Look at Your Hand

What provokes you to worship? Is it the sight of the Grand Canyon or great planets? How about something closer? You can study the genius of God's hand in studying your hand. Look at the palm of your right hand. Study the lines, the unique fingerprints, the way it was created to take a strong grip or touch with tenderness. Think of the nerves of the living skin that allow you to feel warmth, or the blood that constantly flows through your hands. Look at the rigid nails that grow at prearranged curves ... and all this was made from food you have eaten, and all that food traces itself back to the soil. God is so great, so wonderful, so magnificent, so glorious, and when words can't express our thoughts of Him, worship takes over. Okay, stop staring at your hand ... because

There goes another minute.
Gone forever. **Go share your faith while you still have time.**

TICK ...
TICK ...
TICK ...
TICK ...
TICK ...
TICK ...
TICK ...
TICK ...
TICK ...
TICK ...
TICK ...
TICK ...
TICK ...
TICK ...
TICK ...
TICK ...
TICK ...
TICK ...
TICK ...
TICK ...
TICK ...
TICK ...
TICK ...
TICK ...
TICK ...
TICK ...

Out of Control

Moments after a huge earthquake hit Los Angeles in the early hours of a morning in 1994, a traffic officer raced on his bike over a high freeway overpass. Unbeknown to him, the freeway had collapsed in the middle with a fifty-foot drop to the earth below. One moment he was racing across a freeway at 70 MPH on his way to do his duty; the next moment, he was flying through the air on his way to meet his Maker. One moment he was safe and in control; the next moment he had lost control and was at the mercy of a law he had inadvertently violated—the law of gravity. That's how many people enter their eternal destiny. One moment they are speeding down the freeway of sin, and the next moment they are under the control of the Law of sin and death. May God give them light to see their danger.

There goes another minute.
Gone forever. Go share your faith
while you still have time.

TICK ...
TICK ...
TICK ...
TICK ...
TICK ...
TICK ...
TICK ...
TICK ...
TICK ...
TICK ...
TICK ...
TICK ...
TICK ...
TICK ...
TICK ...
TICK ...
TICK ...
TICK ...
TICK ...

Ear-cutting Zeal

When a crowd showed up to arrest Jesus, Peter took a sword and cut off the ear of the High Priest's servant. Those who reach out to the lost using modern evangelistic methods are a little like Peter. They have zeal without knowledge. They are using the Sword of the Spirit to cut off the ears of the world. When someone makes a commitment to Christ without having a knowledge of sin (which comes by the Law), it's not long until they fall away from the faith. The sad fruit of their experience is that they become "Gospel hardened." Their ear is no longer open to the claims of the Gospel. They have been inoculated to the truth. We must make sure that we are never guilty of adulterating the Gospel. We must make sure that we have "sound doctrine," especially when it comes to reaching out to the lost.

There goes another minute.
Gone forever. **Go share your faith while you still have time.**

What Are They Saying?

Jesus asked Peter, "Who do men say that I am?"²⁰³ Peter had heard what people were saying about Jesus. Do *you* know what people are saying about Him? Do you talk to people about Jesus? Some think He was a great teacher. Others think He was a good man with some good ideas. Others hate Him because of what He said. But there are millions who believe He was the Son of God, that He rose from the dead, but they have never repented and trusted in Him for their eternal salvation. How utterly tragic. No doubt, their deception is that they think that they are good enough to go to heaven. They believe in God, in Jesus, and in their own morality as a means of entrance into immortality. May God in His great mercy help us to reach them before they die in their sins.

There goes another minute.
Gone forever. **Go share your faith while you still have time.**

Imagine How it Will Be

The Bible says the Kingdom of Heaven is coming to this earth. Can you imagine how wonderful it will be? Actually, you can't. We have never seen or heard or imagined anything as wonderful as what God has in store for those who love Him.[204] Think of the most beautiful rose, the cutest puppy, the most breathtaking sunset, or the magnificence of a snow-covered mountain. Imagine now that you were there *before* God created those things. There would be no way you could have predicted such a creation; and even though we can see how unspeakably great God is through the creation we see, He says, "Behold, I make all things new." So, never think of Heaven as a kind of spooky home of "departed spirits." It's down to earth, new bodies, utter perfection, and pleasure forevermore. No more pain. No more suffering. No more death.

**There goes another minute.
Gone forever. Go share your faith
while you still have time.**

TICK ... TICK ... TICK ... TICK

Order *The Way of the Master Minute, Book 2*
today! Either stop by your local Christian
bookstore or go online at
www.WayoftheMaster.com.

Until your new book arrives, you can go back
to the first day of this devotional and work
your way forward. Don't let one day go by
without this minute with the Lord.

Footnotes

1. Psalm 119:162
2. Acts 22:21-22
3. Romans 12:1
4. See Ephesians 6:12
5. 1 Peter 5:9
6. John 4:39
7. John 4:16-18
8. John 4:22
9. 2 John 1:9
10. Daniel 12:3
11. Matthew 5:6
12. John 16:8
13. James 4:1
14. Galatians 6:14
15. Acts 13:16
16. Psalm 66:16
17. Psalm 16:6
18. Romans 3:18
19. Romans 3:1-2
20. Hebrews 5:12
21. The Coming Revival
22. 2 Corinthians 5:11
23. Proverbs 19:23
24. 1 Peter 2:11
25. Jude 23
26. Philippians 2:15
27. 2 Peter 3:10
28. Hebrews 12:26
29. Philemon 6
30. 1 Peter 2:15
31. 2 Corinthians 4:18
32. 2 Peter 1:4
33. Romans 2:9
34. Luke 22:42
35. Philippians 4:13
36. Hebrews 13:6
37. Jude 1:3
38. Acts 21:11
39. Matthew 11:11
40. Luke 1:17
41. John 7:46
42. Galatians 3:13
43. Galatians 2:20
44. Revelation 6:15
45. Matthew 9:20-21
46. Matthew 12:36
47. 1 Corinthians 1:21
48. Romans 10:14
49. Isaiah 6:8
50. Proverbs 23:7
51. Jeremiah 17:9
52. 2 Timothy 1:10
53. John 4:34
54. Mark 16:15
55. Luke 6:38
56. 2 Corinthians 3:12
57. Psalm 139:23
58. Romans 12:16
59. Ephesians 1:18
60. John 1:9
61. Psalm 14:1
62. Acts 5:1-10
63. Matthew 5:22
64. 2 Corinthians 4:6
65. 2 Corinthians 4:4
66. Acts 17:31
67. Philippians 3:11
68. 1 Corinthians 16:22
69. Romans 4:20-21
70. 2 Peter 3:9
71. Colossians 4:2, 1 Thessalonians 5:17, Romans 12:12
72. Romans 1:4

73 Hebrews 12:14
74 2 Timothy 2:19
75 Proverbs 15:8
76 Ephesians 6:19
77 Judges 7:3
78 Joshua 14:11
79 Joshua 14:12
80 Ephesians 5:5
81 Job 32:18-19
82 Mark 16:15
83 Jeremiah 4:19
84 2 Timothy 2:4-5
85 Romans 2:8 & 9
86 Proverbs 15:26
87 Hebrews 8:10
88 Mark 16:15
89 Colossians 1:9
90 Acts 1:11
91 Acts 1:11
92 Acts 22:3
93 2 Samuel 12:13
94 Psalm 90:7-8
95 2 Corinthians 5:11
96 Hebrews 2:2
97 See Hebrews 12:28
98 Psalm 119:71,75
99 See Acts 2:24
100 1 Corinthians 2:14
101 2 Chronicles 16:9
102 John 10:10
103 Hebrews 6:19
104 1 Thessalonians 1:5
105 Romans 8:28
106 Romans 4:16
107 Romans 4:20
108 Psalm 145:3
109 Romans 11:33
110 Philippians 4:13
111 Hebrews 1:14
112 1 Samuel 16:6-7
113 Matthew 5:13
114 Acts 8:4
115 Reader's Digest,
November 1999
116 Revelation 21:8
117 Romans 7:7
118 See Luke 13:3
119 If you are not sure
how to do this,
go to
www.Livingwaters.com
and listen to "Hell's
Best Kept Secret."
120 Proverbs 1:25-28
121 The next six readings
have been adapted
from, *How to Win
Souls and Influence
People*, by Ray
Comfort (Bridge
Logos publishers)
122 See *Scientific Facts in
the Bible*, by Ray
Comfort (Bridge
Logos Publishers).
123 Luke 21:33
124 2 Timothy 1:7
125 2 Timothy 1:7
126 Acts 1:8
127 2 Timothy 2:16-19
128 Acts 2:21
129 1 Peter 1:6-8
130 1 Peter 1:17-19
131 Deuteronomy 31:6
132 Psalm 3:6
133 Isaiah 12:2-3
134 1 Corinthians 10:12-14
135 Psalm 5:3

136 John 11:41
137 Jeremiah 20:9
138 Amos 3:8
139 John 9:4
140 1 Corinthians 9:16
141 Hosea 13:14
142 Isaiah 25:8
143 2 Timothy 1:10
144 Revelation 21;4
145 Acts 10:38
146 Acts 4:31
147 Isaiah 64:1-2
148 Philippians 2:15
149 Hebrews 12:2
150 See Romans 8:18
151 1 John 4:18
152 Isaiah 58:1
153 See Romans 2:15
154 Mark 16:15
155 1 Corinthians 9:19
156 Mark 14:40
157 Romans 3:19
158 Daniel 7:9-10
159 Psalm 10:11
160 Romans 2:5-9
161 Hebrews 1:9
162 Isaiah 53:3
163 Jeremiah 9:1-2
164 1 Corinthians 11:1
165 Psalm 119:53
166 Jeremiah 4:19
167 John 8:31-32
168 www.livingwaters.com
169 Jeremiah 9:23-24
170 Acts 7:22
171 Acts 7:24
172 2 Timothy 4:2
173 Philippians 1:27
174 Proverbs 6:23
175 Mark 10:21
176 Mark 9:43-48
177 John 11:26,27
178 Matthew 7:6
179 Hebrews 10:29
180 *Knowledge of the Holy* (Harper Collins) A.W. Tozer
181 1 John 5:21
182 Ephesians 4:18
183 2 Corinthians 4:4
184 See Matthew 23:37
185 Isaiah 45:22
186 Matthew 22:9
187 John 7:37
188 1 Timothy 2:4
189 Revelation 22:17
190 Genesis 8:21
191 Proverbs 6;18
192 Ezekiel 8:12
193 See Romans 10:15
194 Revelation 14:13
195 Exodus 3:14
196 Judges 15:15-16
197 Exodus 16:22-25
198 Romans 7:10
199 Romans 7:12
200 Revelation 14:6
201 Daniel 12:2-3
202 2 Corinthians 6:2
203 Matthew 16:13
204 1 Corinthians 2:9

For a complete list of books, tracts, CDs and
DVDs by Ray Comfort and Kirk Cameron,
see www.WayoftheMaster.com
or call 1(877) 496-8688,
or write to
Living Waters Publications
P.O. Box 1172, Bellflower, CA 90706.
Also, join thousands of students worldwide
in "The School of Biblical Evangelism" —
www.biblicalevangelism.com

Don't miss Kirk Cameron and Ray Comfort's
free monthly email newsletter.
You may also sign up to receive
The Way of the Master Minute
via daily email. Also, listen to
The Way of the Master Radio — details:
www.WayoftheMasterRadio.com